Also by Joel Osteen

Break Out!
Break Out! Journal
Daily Readings from Break Out!
Every Day a Friday
Every Day a Friday Journal
Daily Readings from Every Day a Friday
Fresh Start
Fresh Start Study Guide
I Declare
I Declare Personal Application Guide
The Power of I Am
The Power of I Am Journal
The Power of I Am Study Guide
You Can, You Will
You Can, You Will Journal
Daily Readings from You Can, You Will
Your Best Life Now
Daily Readings from Your Best Life Now
Your Best Life Begins Each Morning
Your Best Life Now Study Guide
Your Best Life Now for Moms
Your Best Life Now Journal
Starting Your Best Life Now

WAKE UP TO
HOPE
devotional

JOEL & VICTORIA OSTEEN

Faith
Words

LARGE PRINT

Scripture quotations noted NKJV are taken from the *New King James Version* of the Bible. Copyright © 1982 by Thomas Nelson, Inc. Used by permission. All rights reserved.

Scripture quotations noted NIV are taken from *The Holy Bible, New International Version® NIV®*. Copyright © 1973, 1978, 1984, 2011 by Biblica, Inc.™ Used by permission. All rights reserved worldwide.

Scripture quotations noted NLT are taken from the *Holy Bible, New Living Translation*, copyright © 1996, 2004, 2007 by Tyndale House Foundation. Used by permission of Tyndale House Publishers, Inc., Carol Stream, Illinois 60188. All rights reserved.

Scripture quotations noted AMPC are from *The Amplified Bible, Classic Edition*. Copyright © 1954, 1958, 1962, 1964, 1965, 1987 by The Lockman Foundation. All rights reserved. Used by permission. (www.Lockman.org)

Scriptures noted ISV are taken from *The Holy Bible: International Standard Version*. Release 2.0, Build 2015.02.09. Copyright © 1995-2014 by ISV Foundation. All rights reserved internationally. Used by permission of Davidson Press, LLC.

Scripture quotations noted ESV are from *The Holy Bible, English Standard Version®*. Copyright © 2001 by Crossway, a publishing ministry of Good News Publishers. All rights reserved.

Scripture quotations noted NASB are from the *New American Standard Bible®*, Copyright © 1960, 1962, 1963, 1968, 1971, 1972, 1973, 1975, 1977, 1995 by The Lockman Foundation. Used by permission.

Scripture quotations noted KJV are from the *King James Version* of the Holy Bible.

Scripture quotations noted ASV are from the *American Standard Version* of the Holy Bible.

Interior design: Koechel Peterson & Associates, Inc., Minneapolis, Minnesota. Literary development by Lance Wubbels Literary Services, LLC.

FaithWords
Hachette Book Group
1290 Avenue of the Americas
New York, NY 10104
www.faithwords.com

Printed in the United States of America

First Edition: April 2016
10 9 8 7 6 5 4 3 2 1

FaithWords is a division of Hachette Book Group, Inc. The FaithWords name and logo are trademarks of Hachette Book Group, Inc.

The Hachette Speakers Bureau provides a wide range of authors for speaking events. To find out more, go to www.hachettespeakersbureau.com or call (866) 376-6591.

The publisher is not responsible for websites (or their content) that are not owned by the publisher.

ISBN: 978-1-4555-6948-9

INTRODUCTION

How you start the day often determines what kind of day you're going to have. When you wake up in the morning, it's easy to lie in bed thinking negative thoughts. *I don't feel like going to work. I don't want to deal with these children. I didn't exercise yesterday.* We don't realize it, but that's setting the tone for a lousy day. Just like a magnet, you draw in what you continually think about.

It's so important at the start of the day to set your mind in the right direction. If you don't set the tone for the day, negative thoughts will set it for you. That's why we've written this devotional, to help you set your mind for a positive, happy, faith-filled day. When you start the day off grateful, thinking about God's goodness, expecting His favor, you're setting the tone for a blessed, productive day. Take a few minutes each morning and read one devotional. It just takes a couple minutes, but it can make a big difference.

When you wake up to hope, you'll not only have a better attitude, but you'll see more of God's blessings and favor.

It's Coming

Today's Scripture

> *"Though it tarries, wait for it;*
> *because it will surely come."*
>
> HABAKKUK 2:3 NKJV

If you will keep God first in everything you do, He promises that He is going to crown your efforts with success. Because you diligently seek Him, a reward is coming. Favor is coming. Good breaks are coming. Promotion is coming. A shift is coming. Healing is coming. Restoration is coming. It may seem as though it's taking a long time; you may feel as though you've been holding on forever, but keep holding on. The promise will be fulfilled through faith and patience.

Waiting doesn't mean to do nothing; it means get prepared. Now is the time to get ready. God doesn't want you to live an average, ordinary life. Because you depend on Him, He is going to increase you. You are going to bear much fruit. He is going to make you more productive. You're going to get more done in less time. He is going to make your life easier and take you where you could not go on your own. It's going to be greater than you ever even dreamed. Get ready because it's coming—every promise you've stood in faith for, every dream He's placed in your heart that you've contended for is coming to fruition in Jesus' Name!

A Prayer for Today

Father, thank You for Your faithfulness and goodness in my life and for crowning my efforts with success. I ask for Your wisdom and direction in every area of my life. I know that through faith and patience I will receive Your promises. I declare the favor is coming, good breaks are coming, restoration is coming, and promotion is coming to me! Help me to be ready; show me what to do so I am in position to receive everything You have prepared for me in Jesus' Name. Amen.

Wake-Up Thought

You must get your hopes up. You don't have to figure out how God is going to solve your problems or bring it to pass. That's His responsibility. Your job is to believe. Your faith will help you overcome your obstacles.

Closer Than You Think

Today's Scripture

> *Do not cast away your confidence, which has great reward.*
>
> HEBREWS 10:35 NKJV

Have you been praying and believing for something that's taking longer than you thought? Many times people can miss God's best simply because they give up before they see their answer come. Don't let that be you! Be encouraged today, your answer is closer than you think. If it seems as though things are getting more difficult, remember, when the intensity heats up, that means you are closer to your victory. It always seems darkest just before the dawn appears.

Remember, you serve a faithful God. Know that He is working behind the scenes on your behalf. Don't cast away your confidence today, because your reward is coming. And just like a new mother forgets about her labor pain when she is finally holding her newborn, you'll forget about your struggle when you are holding your promise.

While you are waiting, keep an attitude of faith and expectancy. Wake up every morning and declare, "I've come too far to give up now. My due season is coming. I will reap my harvest." Stay in faith and be on the lookout because He has promised you victory, and it's closer than you think!

A Prayer for Today

Father in Heaven, thank You that You are my faithful God, and I can depend on You. Today I stand believing that You are working behind the scenes on my behalf. My faith and trust are in You alone. I declare that my due season is coming and I will reap a harvest! I am looking for Your goodness and expecting the victory. Give me Your strength to stand strong until I see Your promises fulfilled in my life in Jesus' Name. Amen.

Wake-Up Thought

You may have had some setbacks, but this is a new day. Your breakthrough is on the way. God is breathing new life into you. If you  *shake off the discouragement, the winds will start blowing once again—not against you, but for you. When you get in agreement with God, He will cause things to shift in your favor and bring your reward.*

The Lord Will Fight for You

Today's Scripture

> *The Lord will fight for you,*
> *and you shall hold your*
> *peace and remain at rest.*
>
> Exodus 14:14 ampc

In life, we're always going to have critics. We'll always have difficult people who try to upset us and steal our peace and joy. But you don't have to respond to every critic. You can decide to take the high road and let God fight your battles for you.

Sometimes, no matter what you say or do, there will be people who aren't going to accept you. They just don't want to be at peace with you. In fact, when Jesus sent out His disciples to certain homes, He told them to always speak peace over those homes. And then He said in effect, "If they don't receive the peace that you're offering, it will come back to you." That tells me that if you will do your best to be at peace with people, even if they won't receive your peace, that peace will just come back to you.

You'll not only get your peace, but you'll get their share as well! That's double for your trouble! When you do the right thing no matter what is happening, God sees it and rewards it.

A Prayer for Today

Father God, I give You all the honor and praise today. I choose to hold my peace and remain at rest. I choose to do the right thing even when the wrong thing is happening. I refuse to allow anything to steal my peace or joy because the joy of the Lord is my strength. I declare that You are giving me double for my trouble. I thank You for fighting for me. Help me to always take the high road and walk in love and peace with others in Jesus' Name. Amen.

Wake-Up Thought

When you respond in love and peace to others who don't accept you and leave it up to God to pay you back, you have the Creator of the universe fighting your battles, arranging things in your favor, going before you, moving the wrong people out of the way. I believe and declare you are going to see God's payback in amazing ways!

The Same Favor

Today's Scripture

> *Jesus Christ is the same yesterday, today, and forever.*
>
> HEBREWS 13:8 NKJV

It's so important to understand the character of God. What He's done for others, He will do for you. The same God who displayed His favor in the Bible is still at work today. God wants to flood you with the same favor that He flooded Joseph, Abraham, and Elijah with. He wants to open new doors, line up supernatural appointments, and bring new increase and provision. The question is, are you ready to receive it? Can you see it with your eyes of faith?

Today, know that our God is the same yesterday, today, and forever. He is with you and for you. Even before you see things turn around, believe that He is working on your behalf. And when He pours out His favor, it won't be just a drizzle; it's going to be a flood—a flood of ideas, a flood of good breaks, a flood of talent. Keep believing, keep hoping, and keep praising, because the same favor that was in the Bible is coming your way!

A Prayer for Today

Father, thank You for Your favor and blessing that is available to me each and every day. I turn my heart and mind toward You, and I am looking for new open doors and supernatural appointments. I declare that a flood is coming to me! A flood of ideas, good breaks, and talent. I submit my ways to You, knowing that You are faithful. I open my heart to receive everything You have in store for me in Jesus' Name. Amen.

Wake-Up Thought

God will bring a flood of opportunities for you to increase your influence in amazing ways. Don't shrink back in fear. Don't be intimidated. You are well able. You are equipped. You are favored. Dare to take those steps of faith and receive all that He has for you.

File It Away

Today's Scripture

LORD, *my heart is not haughty, nor my eyes lofty. Neither do I concern myself with great matters, nor with things too profound for me.*

PSALM 131:1 NKJV

When things happen in your life that you don't plan, do you find yourself trying to reason it all out or look for a "file," so to speak, in your mind to put it in? What happens when you can't reason it out or make sense of it?

Here's the answer: every one of us needs to create a file in our thinking called the "I Don't Understand It" file. When things come up that don't make sense, things that you can't figure out, instead of getting frustrated or confused, put it in your "I Don't Understand It" file and leave it alone. If you go through life trying to figure out why something bad happened or why things didn't work out, it will cause you to become bitter and stuck in life. Part of trusting God means trusting Him when things don't make sense, because we know that His plan is always for good. We have to know that He will reveal all things in His time—even if that means in eternity.

Is there something that didn't make sense that you know you need to file away? Choose to trust God. Choose to keep moving forward. Know that He loves you, He is for you, and He has a great plan for your future!

A Prayer for Today

Father, today I thank You for watching over my life. I surrender my past to You. I surrender my need to have all the answers, and I choose to trust You with all my heart and I will not lean to my own understanding. I refuse to remain stuck because I don't understand everything. I declare that I am moving forward and I ask You to fill me with Your peace. Fill me with Your grace and compassion as I press forward into the victory You have prepared for me in Jesus' Name. Amen.

Wake-Up Thought

Difficulties can make you bitter, or they can make you better. They can drag you down and make you a sour person, or they can inspire you to reach for new heights. Don't waste another minute trying to figure out why certain bad things have happened. If you will stay in an attitude of faith and victory, God has promised that He will turn any emotional wounds around. He'll use them to your advantage, and you will come out better than you would have had they not happened to you.

Give Your Faith a Voice

Today's Scripture

> *And since we have the same spirit of faith, according to what is written, "I believed and therefore I spoke," we also believe and therefore speak.*

2 CORINTHIANS 4:13 NKJV

Every believer has been given a measure of faith. In order to see the promises of God come to pass in your life, you have to give your faith a voice. You must declare what God says about you in His Word. Those seeds of faith inside you are activated when you speak them out into the atmosphere. That's why the Scripture tells us, "Let the weak say, 'I am strong.'" When you give your faith a voice and send forth the Word of God, the Bible says that He watches over His Word to bring it to pass in your life.

Every word you speak is a seed. Don't dig up your seed by speaking against your faith! Don't allow words of defeat or negativity to come out of your mouth. Instead, water your seed by continuing to declare the Word of God. When you wake up every morning, thank Him that His promises are coming to pass in your life. As you do, you will see those things come to pass and live the life of victory God has prepared for you!

A Prayer for Today

Father, I praise You because You are a good and faithful God. Today I humbly come before You submitting my thoughts, my actions, and my words to You.
Show me when I speak words of doubt, discouragement, and negativity so I can change. Help me to give my faith a voice by speaking Your Word daily. May my words and my thoughts be pleasing to You always in Jesus' Name. Amen.

Wake-Up Thought

Words have creative power. When you speak something out, you give life to your faith. One of the best things you can do is take a few minutes every morning and make positive declarations over your life. Declare every day, "I am confident. I am valuable. I am one of a kind. I am a child of the Most High God," and you'll see God release His promises for your life.

Exceptional Favor

Today's Scripture

> *But the path of the [uncompromisingly] just and righteous is like the light of dawn, that shines more and more (brighter and clearer) until [it reaches its full strength and glory in] the perfect day [to be prepared].*
>
> PROVERBS 4:18 AMPC

We all face challenges. We all have obstacles to overcome. But if we can keep the right perspective, it will help us stay in faith so that we can move forward into victory. You may feel right now as though the challenges that you face are too big or too overwhelming. One thing we've learned is that average people have average problems. Ordinary people have ordinary challenges. But remember, you're not average.

You're not ordinary. You are extraordinary. God breathed His life into you. You are exceptional, and exceptional people face exceptional difficulties. But the good news is that we serve an exceptional God! He'll pour out His exceptional grace, exceptional wisdom, and exceptional favor!

When you have an extraordinary problem, instead of being discouraged, be encouraged, knowing that you're an extraordinary person and have an extraordinary future. Your path is shining brighter and brighter. You are on an extraordinary path. Keep standing in faith, keep declaring victory over your future, keep declaring His promises. Keep declaring that you are moving forward into the exceptional favor the Lord has in store for you!

A Prayer for Today

Father in Heaven, I lift my eyes to You and give you all the praise and glory. I know that You are the One who helps me and has given me an extraordinary life. Help me to keep the right perspective and to continue moving forward. I thank You for pouring out Your exceptional grace, exceptional wisdom, and exceptional favor upon my life. I choose to stand in faith today, knowing that You have a wonderful plan in store for me in Jesus' Name! Amen.

Wake-Up Thought

Life will try to push you down and steal your sense of value. Get up every morning and remind yourself of who you are and who your Creator is.  *Your value comes because of whose you are. You are God's masterpiece. You have royalty in your blood. You have exceptional favor on your life in every way. Now put your shoulders back, hold your head up high, and start carrying yourself as a child of the Most High God.*

No Lack

Today's Scripture

> *"For the LORD your God is bringing you into a good land—a land with brooks, streams, and deep springs gushing out into the valleys and hills."*
>
> DEUTERONOMY 8:7 NIV

God has a place prepared for you just like He prepared a place for His people in Scripture. Notice that in this place God has prepared, there is no shortage—no shortage of resources, no shortage of opportunities, no shortage of creativity, of friendships, of joy and peace. In the good land, you will lack no good thing.

Anytime you are tempted to get down or look at what you don't have, turn it around. Say, "Lord, I want to thank You that You are bringing me into my garden, a land of blessing, a land where my gifts and talents will come out to the full, a good land where I will fulfill my destiny, a good land where I'll live healthy, happy, and whole, a good land where my whole house will honor You!"

A Prayer for Today

*Father, I love You and thank You for Your
goodness. Help me to see with eyes of faith
the good land that You have prepared for
me. Thank You for providing for my needs
and that no good thing will You withhold
from me. I proclaim there will be no lack,
no shortage of opportunities, creativity,
friendships, joy, or peace! Help me to walk
in Your ways, to stay close to You, and honor
You in all that I do in Jesus' Name. Amen!*

Wake-Up Thought

*This morning, receive this into your spirit.
God is bringing you into a good land that's
flowing with increase, flowing with good
breaks, flowing with opportunity, where you
not only have enough for yourself, but you're
running over. If you're not in a good and
spacious place, don't settle there. The God
of Abundance will lead you to a good and a
spacious land.*

God Works for Your Good

Today's Scripture

> *And we know that in all things God works for the good of those who love him, who have been called according to his purpose.*
>
> ROMANS 8:28 NIV

God has a plan to take every adversity and every hardship you go through and use it. He's not going to beat you down and make your life miserable. No, God's dream is to take that difficulty and supernaturally turn it around and use it to bring you good. He will use those tough times to bring you out stronger, more mature, and prepared for promotion! Goodness, mercy, and unfailing love are God's plan for you!

You may not understand everything that's going on in your life right now, but stay encouraged and keep your head held high. Know that God is working in your life. Keep being faithful. Keep doing the right thing, knowing that in the end God is going to turn things around in your favor. If God is for you, who can be against you? No one. Greater is the One who is in you than anyone who can be against you. No matter what's going on around you today, you can put a smile on your face because God is working things together for your good because He loves you!

A Prayer for Today

Father in Heaven, I praise You for Your goodness, mercy, and unfailing love for me. Thank You for all You've done for me in my past and for what You are preparing for my future. I trust that You will turn everything around for my good and Your plans. I declare I am coming out stronger, more mature, and prepared for promotion! Help me keep my eyes on You and stand strong as I look for Your goodness all the days of my life in Jesus' Name. Amen.

Wake-Up Thought

God is in complete control. You don't have to get upset when things don't go your way. Quit letting little things steal your joy. Life is too short to live it negative, offended, bitter, and discouraged. Start believing that God is directing your steps. Believe that He is in control of your life. Stay calm and stay in faith; God promised that all things will work out for your good.

I Can

Today's Scripture

> I can do all things through Christ who strengthens me.
>
> PHILIPPIANS 4:13 NKJV

When was the last time you declared "I can" out loud? It's not something people think to do every day. In fact, most people tend to magnify their limitations. They focus on their shortcomings. But Scripture makes it plain: all things are possible to those who believe. That's right! It is possible to see your dreams fulfilled. It is possible to overcome that obstacle. It is possible to climb to new heights. It is possible to embrace your destiny. You may not know how it will all take place. You may not have a plan, but all you have to know is that if God said you can...you can!

Today, why don't you begin to open yourself up to possibilities in your future by simply declaring this verse, "I can do all things through Christ who strengthens me"? At the stoplight, when you're waiting in line, anytime you have a second, just quote this verse to yourself again. Let it sink down deeply into your heart. As you do, His word will transform you. Faith will rise up in your heart and will boldly embrace the blessings that He has in store for you!

A Prayer for Today

Father, I praise You and thank You for empowering me by Your Holy Spirit to do everything that I'm called to do. I will not magnify my shortcomings. I will magnify Your greatness. I know I am not alone because You promised to be with me. I receive Your strength, grace, and mercy to help me today. Thank You for Your hand of blessing on me as I submit my ways to You. I declare "I can" do all things in Jesus' Name! Amen.

Wake-Up Thought

God knows every battle that you will ever face, including every temptation and every obstacle. He has armed you with strength for that battle. He has already equipped you. Quit telling yourself, "This is too much. I can't handle it." Get up in the morning expecting good things, then go through the day positive, focused on your vision, running your race, knowing that you are well able. You can, you will!

Ultimate Victory

Today's Scripture

> *I have told you these things, so that in Me you may have [perfect] peace and confidence. In the world you have tribulation and trials and distress and frustration; but be of good cheer [take courage; be confident, certain, undaunted]! For I have overcome the world. [I have deprived it of power to harm you and have conquered it for you.]*
>
> JOHN 16:33 AMPC

When trials and challenges come, it's easy to feel overwhelmed or discouraged. You may feel lost or uncertain about the future. That's when we need to turn our hearts and minds to God because He has promised that no matter what we face, we can have His perfect peace. We can feel His perfect love. We can have confidence because He has already overcome the world.

The key is that we have to keep an eternal perspective. We have to know that the trials that come our way are only temporary. We may experience tragedy or loss in this life, but with God on our side, we have the ultimate victory in eternity. We may have seasons of grief or sadness here on earth, but He is our Comforter, and in the end, He will wipe away every tear from our eyes.

Remember, when difficulties arise, focus on the fact that you have the ultimate victory. Don't let fear paralyze you; instead, put your faith and hope in God. Those things that the enemy meant for evil, God will turn around for your good. He'll lead you out stronger, wiser, and more alive than ever before.

A Prayer for Today

Heavenly Father, thank You for Your perfect peace and perfect love. I let go of fear, worry, and anxiety today. Even when things don't make sense, I choose to trust You. Even when I don't feel victorious, I know that You are with me and I am always an overcomer. This trial is temporary and You are bringing me out. I choose to put my faith and hope in You today, knowing that You will never disappoint me in Jesus' Name. Amen.

Wake-Up Thought

God does not prevent every negative thing from coming into our lives, because adversities and hardships are opportunities for us to go higher. If we'll stay full of joy and full of hope, when we come out, we'll be more blessed, healthy, and successful, better off than we were previously. We can stay filled with hope, knowing that God will never waste the adversity. He will always use it to our advantage.

He Wants to Surprise You

Today's Scripture

> *If you will listen diligently to the voice of the Lord your God, being watchful to do all His commandments which I command you this day ... all these blessings shall come upon you and overtake you if you heed the voice of the Lord your God.*

DEUTERONOMY 28:1–2 AMPC

A surprise is simply something good that you weren't really expecting. It's something that makes you feel special and lets you know that someone is thinking about you. Surprises bring us joy and lift our hearts. Your God wants to surprise you and overtake you with His goodness. He wants to do things that make your life easier and lets you know how much He loves you.

God wants to catch you by surprise! He wants to help you accomplish your dreams and overcome your obstacles. He wants to amaze you with His goodness and mercy. We should wake up every morning with the attitude, *I can't wait to see what God is going to do today!*

Make room in your heart and mind for what God wants to do in your life today. Keep an attitude of faith and expectancy. As you do, you'll see His surprises. You'll see God's hand of blessing overtake you and bring you to new levels in every area of your life!

A Prayer for Today

Father in Heaven, thank You for Your loving care toward me. I can't wait to see what You are going to do today! I open my heart and mind to You right now. Fill me with Your goodness and overtake me with Your blessings. I desire to please You in every area of my life. Help me maintain an attitude of faith and expectancy. I declare I will accomplish my dreams and overcome every obstacle. I am looking for Your surprises! I honor You today and give You all the glory in Jesus' Name. Amen.

Wake-Up Thought

One translation of Deuteronomy 28:2 says that when you are honoring God, "You will become a magnet for blessings." That means you are attracting the goodness of God. When you keep God in first place, favor is overtaking you, promotion is headed your way, divine connections are searching you out. Suddenly, your health improves or a good break comes. That's not a coincidence. That's the commanded blessing on your life.

Say "I Can" to the Mountain

Today's Scripture

> *And Jesus answered them, Truly I say to you, if you have faith (a firm relying trust) and do not doubt, you will not only do what has been done to the fig tree, but even if you say to this mountain, Be taken up and cast into the sea, it will be done.*

MATTHEW 21:21 AMPC

We've all had seasons when the challenges of life feel overwhelming. During those times, it's easy to be tempted to talk about how bad things are. Maybe you received a bad medical report, or maybe you're facing a financial obstacle. The more you talk about something, the bigger it becomes in your mind.

Instead, you have to dig your heels in and say, "No, I am not going to give life to that defeat. I am not going to speak sickness over myself. I'm not going to speak lack. I'm not going to speak fear. I'm choosing a different report. I believe the report of the Lord that says, 'I can do all things through Christ.' I can defeat this sickness. I can break this addiction. I can have peace in my home. I can see restoration in my relationships."

Remember, even if you don't see how things could ever work out, God does. You have to speak His Word over those mountains in your life and declare favor over those situations. Instead of talking to God about how big your problems are, talk to your problems about how big your God is! As you speak to your mountains, they will be moved, and you will walk forward into the victory God has prepared for you!

A Prayer for Today

Father, thank You for Your strength and comfort in difficult times. I refuse to be overwhelmed, because You are helping me and You hold victory in store for me. I declare that I can do all things through Christ who gives me strength. I serve a mighty God! I speak to the mountains in my life and say, "Be moved!" Thank You, Father, for Your blessings, favor, and victory over my future in Jesus' Name. Amen!

Wake-Up Thought

There was a man in the Scripture name Zerubbabel. He faced a huge mountain. To rebuild the temple in Jerusalem was a big obstacle with enemies opposing every step. But he didn't talk about how impossible it was. He said, "Who are you, O great mountain, that would stand before me? You shall become a mere molehill." He was prophesying his future, declaring "I can defeat you!"

Thank Him in Advance

Today's Scripture

> Though the fig tree may not blossom, nor fruit be on the vines… yet I will rejoice in the LORD, I will joy in the God of my salvation.
>
> HABAKKUK 3:17–18 NKJV

We all have dreams and goals that God has placed in our hearts, things we're believing for, situations we're praying will turn around. These promises start off like seeds. They don't come to pass overnight. There's always a period of waiting involved. From the time we pray till the time we see it come to fulfillment, that's called "the trial of our faith." This is when many people get discouraged and give up. They start believing the negative thoughts, *It's never going to happen. It's taken too long.* Now, that seed is lying there dormant, but it's still alive. It still has potential. You have to do your part and start watering the seed. The way you water it is by thanking God in advance and declaring His Word. You can't wait until you receive the promise. You have to thank God that the answer is on the way!

Today, no matter what you are facing, know that God is greater than all of it. He has the answer and is working for your good behind the scenes. All through the day say, "Father, thank You that whatever I touch prospers and succeeds. Thank You that Your favor surrounds me like a shield." Thank God in advance, water those seeds of faith, and take hold of every promise He has for you!

A Prayer for Today

Father, I love You and praise You today. I choose to rejoice in You, knowing that victory is on the way. No matter what my circumstances look like, I know You  *are greater than my circumstances. You are greater than all! I declare You are bringing my dreams and desires to pass. I trust that You are working behind the scenes to fulfill every one of Your promises in Jesus' Name. Amen.*

Wake-Up Thought

Don't believe the enemy's negative lies. Keep being faithful, keep moving forward, keep honoring God in all you do. Start thanking God that He is in control, thanking Him that He is fighting your battles, thanking God that new doors are opening, thanking Him that no weapon formed against you will prosper. Be content in the watering season, for the harvest is coming!

Strong Against Difficulty

Today's Scripture

> *"Do not fear, for I am with you; do not be dismayed, for I am your God. I will strengthen you and help you; I will uphold you with my righteous right hand."*
>
> ISAIAH 41:10 NIV

It's easy to look around at what's happening in the world today and be tempted to feel afraid or dismayed. Circumstances may seem overwhelming. Maybe your business is struggling, maybe you lost your job, maybe you're struggling in a relationship or concerned about the economy. During times like these, it's important to remember that God has promised that He will never leave us nor forsake us. In fact, not only is He with us, He has promised to strengthen us and harden us to difficulties. That means, when tough times come, they just bounce right off of you. You don't allow your circumstances to steal your peace and joy. You have the attitude that says, *This may be a big problem, but my God is bigger!*

Keep in mind that the enemy isn't after your checkbook; he's ultimately after your peace and joy. He knows that if he can get your joy, he can get your strength. But when you stay connected to the Father through prayer, studying the Word and declaring His promises over your life, you'll be hardened to difficulties and stay safe in the palm of God's hand!

A Prayer for Today

Father, thank You for Your strength and mercy in times of difficulties. Today I let go of fear and I refuse to let anything steal my joy. I trust in You, because You are upholding me with Your righteous hand. I know You have a plan of victory for me. Fill me with Your supernatural joy and peace. Thank You for keeping me close to You in the palm of Your hand in Jesus' Name. Amen.

Wake-Up Thought

This morning, step back and see your life from a new perspective. Realize that God has you in the palm of His hand. Enter into this rest. He knows where you are. If something difficult comes your way, you can handle it. The prophet Isaiah said, "Take hold of His strength." Get up every morning and remind yourself, "I'm ready for and equal to anything that comes my way. I am strong."

Sharpen Your Skills

Today's Scripture

> *"He has filled them with skill to do all manner of work."*
>
> EXODUS 35:35 NKJV

I t's easy to fall into "destination disease." That's when you're comfortable with where you are. You're not stretching, not learning anything new. There is nothing wrong with being happy where you are, but you have to remember that you have so much more inside of you. You were created to increase, to grow, to stretch and sharpen your skills.

Studies tell us that the average person only uses 11 percent of their brain. Think about how much more potential we all could be tapping into. Maybe you're an accountant. That's good, but don't settle there. Why don't you go get your CPA license? There's a new skill you can develop. That gift will make more room for you. Maybe you're an electrician, a mechanic, a plumber. That's great, but what steps are you taking to improve? In this day and age, if you are at the same skill level today as you were five years ago, you're at a disadvantage.

Today, shake out of that "destination disease" and start sharpening your skills. Keep stretching, keep growing, and keep moving forward into the life of blessing God has prepared for you!

A Prayer for Today

Father, I praise You for every good and perfect gift that You have given me. I offer my life to You as a living sacrifice to do Your will. I desire to honor You with every gift and every talent You have given me. Show me how to sharpen my skills, improve my talents, and increase to new levels. Help me to have a spirit of excellence and always bring glory and honor to You in Jesus' Name. Amen.

Wake-Up Thought

God is bringing about new seasons of growth in your life. He will stir you out of your comfortable situations and lead you into situations that make you stretch your faith. God has something better in front of you—new doors of opportunity, new relationships, and new levels of favor. It may be uncomfortable, but God loves you too much to just leave you alone.

At Any Moment

Today's Scripture

> "Behold, I make a covenant. Before all your people I will do marvels such as have not been done in all the earth, nor in any nation; and all the people among whom you are shall see the work of the LORD. For it is an awesome thing that I will do with you."
>
> EXODUS 34:10 NKJV

God said, "I'm going to do great things that I have never done before anywhere on earth. People will see what great things I can do because I'm going to do something awesome for you." Now when God uses the word *awesome*, He is not talking about a trickle, a stream, or a river of power. He is talking about a flood of favor, a flood of ideas, a flood of healing. It may not look like it in the natural right now; but remember, you're under a Flash Flood Warning. Any moment, the heavens could open up. Any moment, you could meet the right person. Any moment, God could do something awesome, something that you've never seen before in your life.

Now the real question is, will you let this seed take root? Every voice will tell you why this is not for you, but God wants to do something amazing in your life. Why don't you get into agreement with Him and say, "God, this is for me today. I'm raising my expectations. I'm shaking off doubt, negativity, disappointment, self-pity, little dreams, and little goals. God, I'm going to make room for a flood of Your goodness!"

A Prayer for Today

Father, I love You and give You all the praise today! I believe that You want to do something amazing in my life. I surrender my thoughts, words, and attitudes to You. I am shaking off doubt, negativity, disappointment, and self-pity. I am expecting a flood of Your favor, ideas, healing, and restoration. My eyes are on You, and I declare I will see You do marvelous and awesome things in my life. Have Your way in me and overwhelm me with Your goodness in Jesus' Name! Amen.

Wake-Up Thought

Conditions are just right. You've honored God. You've been faithful. You've passed the test. Now God is saying: "You need to get ready. There's about to be a flood of My goodness, a flood of opportunity, a flood of good breaks, to where you are overwhelmed with the surpassing greatness of My favor. You will rise to a level that you could have never reached on your own. It's beyond your expectations. It puts you into overflow."

When God Opens the Floodgates

Today's Scripture

And He led them on safely, so that they did not fear; but the sea overwhelmed their enemies.

PSALM 78:53 NKJV

Nothing can stop the force of mighty rushing water. Three or four feet of water can pick up a car that weighs thousands of pounds and move it all around. You've probably seen news reports where whole houses are being swept away during a huge flood or cities in a tidal wave.

In the same way, you may have obstacles that look insurmountable and dreams that look unattainable, but let me encourage you: when God releases a flood of His power, nothing will be able to stop you. That sickness may look big, but when God releases a flood of healing, it doesn't stand a chance. Your opposition may be stronger, better financed, and better equipped, but when God opens up the floodgates, they'll be no match for you.

You may not have the connections or resources you need, but when God releases a flood of favor, people will come out of the woodwork to help you. Good breaks, opportunity, the right people will search you out. You need to get ready not for a trickle, not for a stream, not for a river, but for a flood of God's favor, a tidal wave of God's goodness. A tsunami of His increase is coming your way!

A Prayer for Today

Father, I love You and thank You for Your mighty power at work in my life. I am not moved by any obstacles in my way because I know You  *are greater than anything I may be facing. I know that no weapon formed against me will prosper. I believe that Your floodgates are open, and a tidal wave of Your goodness is wiping out my enemies and clearing the way for victory in every area of my life in Jesus' Name. Amen.*

Wake-Up Thought

When King David faced an impossible situation in battle, he asked God for help. God gave him such an overwhelming victory that he said, "God has broken my enemies...like the bursting forth of water." He named the place Baal-Perazim, which means, "the God of the breakthrough." When the God of the breakthrough shows up and releases His power in your life, it will be like the bursting forth of waters.

Help Is on the Way

Today's Scripture

> "With us is the LORD our
> God, to help us and to fight
> our battles."
>
> 2 CHRONICLES 32:8 NKJV

We've learned that when the enemy attacks, God reacts. God doesn't just sit back and think, *Well, I wonder what's going to happen. I wonder what they're going to do.* No, God goes to work. You are His most prized possession. It says in Psalms, "God is close to those who are hurting. God is close to the brokenhearted."

God knows when you've gotten a bad medical report. He knows when you're struggling in your finances. He knows when you're being mistreated. You may not see anything happening, but you can be assured that Almighty God is not only aware, He is at work. He already has the solution. If you will stay in faith, at the right time, He will release a flood of His power, a flood of healing, a flood of restoration. He will not only bring you out, He will bring you out better off than you were before!

A Prayer for Today

Father, thank You for being my help, my refuge, and my strength. I know that You are with me even in the hard times, even when I can't see a way out. I believe You will make a way where there seems to be no way. You already have the solution. I trust that You are working behind the scenes in my life and will bring me through to victory in Jesus' Name. Amen.

Wake-Up Thought

What are you expecting from God? What are you believing for? Would you release your faith for something big? It doesn't matter who likes you or who doesn't like you. All that matters is God likes you. He accepts you. He approves of you. His favor surrounds you like a shield. Promotion doesn't come from people. It comes from God. If you'll be bold enough to believe big, He will fight your battles.

It Is Finished

Today's Scripture

> *I am certain that God, who began the good work within you, will continue his work until it is finally finished on the day when Christ Jesus returns.*
>
> PHILIPPIANS 1:6 NLT

I t's interesting that the last thing Jesus said on the cross was, "It is finished." It certainly looked like the end. It looked as though it was over. But maybe that wasn't just a statement of fact; it was a statement of faith. Jesus was saying to His Father, "I've done My part. I've fulfilled My destiny. Now I have total trust and confidence that You are going to finish what You started." Even though it looked like the end, in reality, it was only the beginning.

When it looks dark in your life, when things aren't going your way, dare to make that declaration of faith just like Jesus, "It is finished." What you're really saying is, "God, I know You are going to turn this situation around. I know You are going to heal my body. I know You are going to restore my family. I know You are going to give me the breaks that I need. I've done my part, and I know You will do Yours." Always remember to speak victory over your circumstances because He is faithful, and He will complete what He's started in you.

A Prayer for Today

Father, I give You all the praise and glory. Thank You for Your faithfulness to me. I thank You that You will complete what You've started in my life. Today I choose to put my trust in You, knowing that a shift is coming. I declare You are turning my situation around! I pray that Your will be done in every area of my life in Jesus' Name! Amen.

Wake-Up Thought

God is called "the author and the finisher of our faith." He has not only given you the grace to start; He has given you the grace to finish. When you are tempted to get discouraged, give up on a dream, give up on a relationship, or give up on a project, you have to remind yourself, I was not created to give up. I was not created to quit. I was created to finish.

Hope

Do not cast away your
confidence, which
has great reward.

HEBREWS 10:35 NKJV

Undeserved, Unearned, Unexplainable

Today's Scripture

> *Whoever finds me finds life, and obtains favor from the LORD.*
>
> PROVERBS 8:35 NKJV

God loves you and He is for you! He is for your good; He is for your success; He is for your future. He desires for you to have every blessing and every promise declared in His Word. This is what the Bible calls His favor. At some point in our lives, even if we didn't recognize it, we have all experienced God's favor. It is simply His undeserved, unearned, unexplainable goodness in your life. God's favor causes you to reap where you haven't sown. His favor protects you, promotes you, and opens new doors. His favor takes you places you could never go on your own.

Today, declare over your life that God is going to unleash His unprecedented favor on you—favor like you've never seen before! The key is to stay connected to Him—stay in fellowship with Him through prayer, worship, and reading His Word. Let Him direct your steps and mold and shape your character. He'll pour out His grace, mercy, and supernatural, undeserved, unearned, unexplainable favor on every area of your life!

A Prayer for Today

Father God, thank You for Your mercy and divine protection in my life. I trust that You are working behind the scenes on my behalf. I know that Your plans are to prosper me and give me a hope and a future. I declare that You are unleashing Your unprecedented favor upon my life! I set my mind and heart on You this day and expect to see Your goodness in Jesus' Name. Amen.

Wake-Up Thought

You need to get a revelation of how much your Heavenly Father is longing to be good to you. Sometimes we think, God has bigger things to deal with than me getting this business off the ground or taking this trip to see my relatives. I can't bother God with that. No, it's just the opposite. God is the one who puts the dream in your heart, and He wants to amaze you with His goodness.

No Limits

Today's Scripture

> I have seen that everything [human]
> has its limits and end [no matter how
> extensive, noble, and excellent]; but
> Your commandment is exceedingly
> broad and extends without limits
> [into eternity].
>
> PSALM 119:96 AMPC

We serve a supernatural God! He can do what medicine cannot do. He is not limited by your education, your background, or the family you came from. He's not moved by the things people have spoken over you. He's not up in Heaven all frantic, trying to figure out how to get you to your destiny. He knows the end from the beginning. He already has solutions to problems you've not even had. He is all powerful and all knowing. People may have tried to push you down, but if you'll just remove the labels that people hang on you and get into agreement with God, He will push you up. He will take you where you could not go on your own.

You don't have to figure it all out. All God asks you to do is believe. When you believe, all things are possible. When you believe, doors will open that should have never opened. When you believe, God will take you from the back to the front. Don't let negative labels hold you down. Remember, we serve a God who knows no limits! Get in step with Him and live your life without limits, too!

A Prayer for Today

Father, I praise You because You are all powerful and all knowing. I ask You to help me take the limits off my life. I let go of old mindsets and negative labels and commit to renew my mind by meditating on Your powerful words. I declare I am increasing in faith and in the knowledge of Your Word. Thank You for transforming me into Your likeness in Jesus' Name. Amen.

Wake-Up Thought

God is not limited by our education, by our nationality, or by our background. But He is limited by our thinking. If you think you've reached  *your limits, you have. If you think you'll never get well or get out of debt, you won't. You have to change your thinking. It doesn't matter how impossible it looks. Our God is not limited to the natural. All the forces of darkness cannot stop what our supernatural God wants to do.*

His Mercy Is Greater

Today's Scripture

> *For the LORD is good; His mercy is everlasting, and His truth endures to all generations.*
>
> PSALM 100:5 NKJV

When you make a mistake, unfortunately, the critics and naysayers come out of the woodwork. People will tell you, "You're all washed up. It's too late." If you wear that label, it will keep you from the amazing future God has in store. God says, "My mercy is bigger than any mistake." God says, "I can still get you to your destiny." God says, "I will give you beauty for those ashes. I'll pay you back double for the unfair things that have happened." You wouldn't be alive unless God had another victory in your future. Why don't you take off the "washed up" label? Take off the "failure," "guilty," "condemned" labels and put on some new labels: "redeemed," "restored," "forgiven," "bright future," "new beginning."

Always remember, you have been made in the image of Almighty God. God did not make any mistakes. You are the perfect size. You have the right personality, the right gifts, the right looks, and the right skin color. You are not an accident. God designed you precisely for the race that is laid out for you. You are fully equipped for this life, and His mercy is greater than any mistake you could make. Embrace the truth and the victory He has in store for your future!

A Prayer for Today

*Father, I love You and thank You for Your
great mercy. Thank You for equipping me
for everything I need in this life. I choose
to reject old labels and to forgive those
who have hurt me. I will not listen to the
naysayers, but I will believe what You say
about me. I declare I am forgiven, anointed,
accepted, and approved by You! I set my eyes
on You, Jesus, the Author and Finisher of
my faith in Jesus' Name. Amen.*

Wake-Up Thought

*The Scripture says that God's mercies are new
every morning. You may have made a lot of
mistakes, but God has not run out of mercy. He
makes a fresh new batch every single morning.
Do you know why? Because He knew we were
going to use up all that He made yesterday!
Don't carry around yesterday's mistakes any
longer. Simply receive God's mercy and
forgiveness. Today is a new beginning.*

You're on Assignment

Today's Scripture

> We are therefore Christ's ambassadors, as though God were making his appeal through us. We implore you on Christ's behalf: Be reconciled to God.
>
> 2 CORINTHIANS 5:20 NIV

God has an assignment for you that nobody else can fulfill. God needs you. He needs your gifts, your smile, your love, your passion. You are a part of His divine plan. You have something to offer that nobody else can offer. Nobody has your exact personality, your exact looks. There is something unique about you. Don't wear that "average" label. If you think you're average, you'll be average. If you think you're ordinary, you'll live an ordinary, "get by" life and never do anything great.

The truth is, there is nothing ordinary about you. You have the fingerprints of God all over you. The Creator of the universe breathed His life into you. He crowned you with His favor. You have royal blood flowing through your veins. You have a destiny to fulfill, something greater than you've ever imagined. Embrace His truth, embrace His love, and embrace the blessings He has in store for your future!

A Prayer for Today

Father, thank You for equipping me and choosing me to be Your ambassador, Your representative on this earth. I choose to live an extraordinary life, not just an average life. I declare that I have Your royal blood flowing through my veins and I have a great destiny to fulfill! Help me to be Your light and to use my gifts and talents to lead others to know You in Jesus' Name. Amen.

Wake-Up Thought

God made you as you are on purpose. Nothing about you is by accident. Start to declare, "God has called me to represent Him in this world." You talk like that and you won't have that weak, defeated, "I'm just average" mentality. You'll carry yourself like an ambassador. Not in pride, but with a quiet knowing that you've been handpicked by the Creator of the universe and you have something amazing to offer this world.

Passing the Small Tests

Today's Scripture

> *If anyone, then, knows the good they ought to do and doesn't do it, it is sin for them.*
>
> JAMES 4:17 NIV

Many people expect the voice of God to boom like a loudspeaker, but Scripture tells us that He speaks in a still, small voice. To us, it seems like an impression inside.

We think, *I know I should go visit my parents. I know I shouldn't eat so many sweets. I know I should stay home and do my schoolwork.* The "I know"s are God talking to us. Don't ignore Him. Learn to be quick to obey.

A lot of times we know what we should do, but we make excuses and reason it out. "I'll do it later. I'm busy now." But we have to understand that God doesn't ask us to do it for His sake. He asks us to do it for our own sake.

We've learned that before God will release big blessings, He will give us small tests. Too often we dismiss it and think, *Oh, that's no big deal.* But if we don't pass these small tests, it will keep us from the big things God has in store.

Today, don't put off the little things that you know you should be doing any longer. Take a step of faith and obey Him. As you're faithful in the little things and pass the small tests, He'll lead you into the greater things He has in store for you.

A Prayer for Today

Father, I praise You for loving me and for speaking to my heart. Thank You for leading me in the path of blessing and directing my steps. Help me to be sensitive to Your voice and to be quick to obey. I desire to pass the small tests so You can trust me with the greater things You have prepared for me in Jesus' Name. Amen.

Wake-Up Thought

The Scripture says, "It's the little foxes that spoil the vines." Many people do not enjoy God's favor as they should, because they don't pass the small tests. Being excellent and honoring God in the small things means you don't compromise. You don't just do what everyone else is doing. Even if everyone else is late, cuts corners, or is undisciplined, you go the extra mile. Make the choice to be excellent.

Let Go of the Wrong Relationships

Today's Scripture

> Do not be misled: "Bad company corrupts good character."
>
> 1 CORINTHIANS 15:33 NIV

D o you ever get around a certain person and feel uneasy or unrest? Something inside says, "Stay away. That's trouble." Those are not just bad vibes. That's the Holy Spirit warning you. It may be small, but it can keep you from a big heartache. You might say, "If I don't hang out with them, I may not have any friends." No, God will give you new friends. He will give you better friends. The key is: if you don't let go of the wrong people, the right people won't show up. This is not talking about a relationship already committed in marriage, but relationships outside of marriage. God doesn't force us to let go of wrong relationships. He has given us our own free will. But when God asks you to give something up, He is never trying to take something away. He is trying to get something better to you. As you obey Him, you grow and mature, which opens the door for more of His blessings and favor.

Remember, bad company corrupts good character. Let go of friends or influences that you know are dragging you down. Trust God to bring the right people and connections across your path. Let go of wrong relationships and move forward in the blessing He has prepared for you!

A Prayer for Today

Father, I love You and worship You today. Thank You for directing my steps and connecting me with godly people. I ask that You help me choose right relationships. Give me courage to let go of the wrong relationships so I can make room for the right relationships You have ordained for my life. I declare You are bringing the right people and connections across my path in Jesus' Name. Amen.

Wake-Up Thought

The only thing that keeps some people from a new level of their destiny is wrong friendships. Beware of associating  *with or adopting the attitudes of people who, through their negative outlook and lack of self-esteem, will rob you of the greatness that God has for you. You cannot hang out with chickens and expect to soar like an eagle. This is what it says in Proverbs: when you walk with wise men, you will become wise.*

Obey Quickly

Today's Scripture

> *"To obey is better than sacrifice."*
>
> 1 SAMUEL 15:22 NIV

One of the best things we can learn in life is to obey God quickly. When God asks you to do it, do it right then. When God told David to go face Goliath, the Bible says David ran to the battlefield. Do you know why? If David would have thought about it long enough, he would have talked himself out of it. If he had gone over all the facts, figures, how much bigger Goliath was, and how much more experience Goliath had, David would have lost his courage and missed his destiny.

When God asks you to do something, don't overanalyze it. Don't reason it out. If you think about it too long, you can miss your destiny. Don't think, *Why should I buy their dinner?*

They've got more money than I do. Or, *Why should I apologize? I apologized first last time.* Or, *Why should I be good to them? They're not being good to me.* No, quit making excuses. Quit reasoning it out. Quit thinking that you heard God wrong and just do it. Learn to be quick to obey and open the door for the blessing God has in store for you!

A Prayer for Today

Father, thank You for goodness and mercy. Today I choose to obey You quickly. Help me not to overthink things, but to trust Your leading in my life, because I know You want what is best. I trust that You are good and desire good things for me. Thank You for ordering my steps and protecting me. Thank You for doing a work in me and through me in Jesus' Name. Amen.

Wake-Up Thought

The Scripture says that if we are willing and obedient, we will eat the best from the land. In other words, we will have the best this life has to offer and more! But God says we have to be willing to obey. Dare to step out of your comfort zone today. God has so much more in store. Keep listening to God, keep pursuing and obeying, and keep believing.

The Blessing Follows Obedience

Today's Scripture

If you fully obey the LORD your God and carefully follow all his commands I give you today, the LORD your God will set you high above all the nations on earth. All these blessings will come on you and accompany you if you obey the LORD your God.

DEUTERONOMY 28:1–2 NIV

God rewards the people who seek after Him. Every time you obey His Word, His blessing will follow. If you learn to obey Him in the small things, if you learn to pass the small tests, there's no limit to how high God will take you. The Scripture says, "When we fully obey God, blessings will chase us down and overtake us." You can't outrun the good things of God.

Always remember, when you obey God in the small things, He will release big blessings. He has big opportunities and new levels of favor, healing, restoration, vindication, and promotion planned in your future. As you stay faithful to Him, you're going to step into the fullness of your destiny and be all that God has created you to be!

A Prayer for Today

Father, today I bless and lift You up because You are worthy to be praised. I dedicate myself to You afresh and anew. My desire is to obey You even in the small things. I declare that I will stay faithful to You and step into the fullness of my destiny! Keep me close to You and help me see Your goodness as I obey Your Word and honor You in all that I do in Jesus' Name. Amen.

Wake-Up Thought

Remember, our lives are an open book before God. He looks into our hearts. God sees every time you go the extra mile to do what's right. He also sees the times when you compromise and take the easy way out. When you hear the alarm go off in your conscience, don't ignore it. Do what you know in your heart is the right thing. Live this day to please God and His blessings will overtake you.

Receive Double

Today's Scripture

> *"Instead of your shame you shall have double honor, and instead of confusion they shall rejoice in their portion. Therefore in their land they shall possess double; everlasting joy shall be theirs."*
>
> ISAIAH 61:7 NKJV

In the Old Testament when this Scripture was written, God's people were going through a very dark time. They were being held captive and mistreated by other nations. God sent this word to encourage them and give them hope for their future, and when the time came, God was faithful to His Word!

Are you going through a difficult time today? Let this word bring you encouragement, too. God wants to give you double for your trouble. He is the God of restoration—that means He's not going to just repay you for every wrong done to you, He's going to go above and beyond and make things even better than they were before.

If you are facing challenges today or going through a time of adversity, remember, it's always darkest just before the dawn appears. Your days are destined to shine brighter because God is faithful. As you stay in faith and are obedient to His Word, you'll receive double for your trouble and see His promises come to pass!

A Prayer for Today

Father, thank You for Your Word that lights my path and guides my steps. I choose to put my trust and hope in You today. I let go of discouragement, because I know that the path of the just gets brighter and brighter. I believe double is coming to me! Thank You for bringing restoration into my life as I keep my heart and mind fixed on You in Jesus' Name. Amen.

Wake-Up Thought

When you face trouble or somebody does you wrong, instead of getting discouraged, your attitude should be, Father, I thank You that I'm now in position to receive double. I know I'm going to come out stronger, healthier, and happier than I've ever been. You are not simply a survivor, you are "more than a conqueror." You don't just defeat the enemy, you gather up all the spoils and are blessed to overflowing.

He'll Make Up for Lost Time

Today's Scripture

> *"I will repay you for the years the locusts have eaten."*
>
> JOEL 2:25 NIV

God knows how to make up for years you've lost in your life. No, you can't relive your childhood, but God can make the rest of your life so rewarding, so fulfilling, that you don't even miss what didn't happen in the past. You may feel as though you wasted years in a relationship that didn't work out. But God can bring somebody into your life so great, so fun, so friendly, so attractive that you won't even remember the years that you've lost. You may have spent years on a job that turned out to be a dead end. You were working your way to the top; things didn't turn out as you had hoped, and now it looks as though it was all a big waste of time. You may not see how you could ever get to where you want to be, but don't believe those lies.

God knows how to make up for lost time. God can accelerate things. God can bring opportunities back across your path that you missed that will thrust you years ahead. It may not have happened the first time, but God will always give you another chance. He'll make up for the lost time and bring you out better and stronger than ever before!

A Prayer for Today

Father, I praise You for being my Redeemer. You are a God of second chances and can make up for lost time. Thank You for Your promise to restore to me the years that have been lost or wasted. I receive this promise by faith. I will not live in regret over the past, but in faith, knowing that You are faithful. I put my trust and hope in You and believe that my best days are out ahead of me in Jesus' Name. Amen.

Wake-Up Thought

God isn't limited to taking you logically from A to B to C. Sometimes God will take you from A to B to C, and then  *thrust you all the way down to S, T, U, V. What happened? You hit a set time fixed by Him that pushed you years ahead. Quit worrying about the past and just run your race. Be the best you can be, and God will get you to where you're supposed to be right on time.*

Dare to Ask

Today's Scripture

> *Now all glory to God, who is able, through his mighty power at work within us, to accomplish infinitely more than we might ask or think.*
>
> EPHESIANS 3:20 NLT

When was the last time you asked God to do something impossible, something out of the ordinary? Sometimes the reason we don't see God do great things is because we only ask Him for small things. Most people pray over their food, pray for protection, or pray for wisdom. That's all good, but don't limit what God can do. There should be something you're praying about, something that you're asking for that is beyond you, something that you can't accomplish in your own strength. Do you dare to ask?

Your dreams may look impossible. You don't have the funding or the connections, but God is saying, "I dare you to ask Me to bring it to pass. I dare you to ask Me to show you a flood of My favor."

All through the Scripture, we see people doing this. Elijah prayed that it wouldn't rain, and for three and a half years there was no rain. Joshua prayed for more daylight, and God stopped the sun. Follow their example and step out in faith. Dare to ask, dare to believe God, and see His mighty hand move on your behalf!

A Prayer for Today

Father, today I give praise and glory to You because You are worthy, You are able, and You are at work in me. Thank You for putting dreams and desires in my heart. I dare to ask for the impossible! Show me Your mighty flood of power! I believe that You can accomplish infinitely more than I could ever ask or think in Jesus' Name. Amen.

Wake-Up Thought

If you dare to believe God, He will line things up for you in ways that are going to boggle your mind. He's already put your name on them. What's your part? Worry? Try to make it happen? Manipulate this person, and maybe they'll do you a favor? No, you don't have to play up to people, hoping they'll throw you a crumb. You are not a beggar; you are a child of the Most High God.

Get Back Up

Today's Scripture

> *"Arise, shine, for your light has come, and the glory of the* LORD *rises upon you."*
>
> ISAIAH 60:1 NIV

Are you going through a tough time today? Are you sitting on the sidelines of life? God is saying, "Arise and get back in the game." If a friend betrayed you, don't go through life lonely. Go out and find some new friends. The right people are in your future. If you lost your job, don't sit around complaining. Go out and find another job. When one door closes, God will always open another door. If you're facing a health issue, fighting that sickness, don't give up on life and start planning your funeral. Arise from that discouragement!

When God sees you do your part, He will do His part. He will give you a new life. That means He will restore your health, give you new opportunities, new relationships. He will give you a new perspective. You will see that even though it's painful, it is not the end. Even though it was unfair, it is not over.

There is still life after the sickness, life after the divorce, life after the bad break. A full life is still in front of you. Today, arise and let God's glory shine all over you!

A Prayer for Today

Father, I love You and thank You for Your grace and mercy on my life. I choose to rise up out of discouragement and put my trust in You. I am getting back in the game and moving forward into the bright future You have for me. Thank You, Lord, for accomplishing Your purposes in my life in Jesus' Name. Amen.

Wake-Up Thought

Some people don't realize they are dragging the pains of the past into the present. It's almost as though they get up each day and fill a big wheelbarrow with junk from the past and bring it into the new day. Let go of that stuff! Put your foot down and make a decision that you will no longer live as a prisoner to your past. God has a bright future in store for you.

He Makes Everything New

Today's Scripture

> *He who was seated on the throne said, "I am making everything new!"*
>
> REVELATION 21:5 NIV

Can you remember the time when you first discovered a big dream in your heart? Maybe you were determined to excel in your career, excel as a parent, or even excel in your walk with the Lord. You probably started out strong, but maybe things got a little difficult and didn't happen as quickly as you would have liked. At that point many people decide, *Let's just settle here. It's not exactly what we wanted, but it's good enough.*

Remember that you were made for more than good enough! Maybe things haven't worked out the way you planned, but now is not the time to stop and settle. Now is the time to dig your heals in and begin again. And even if that dream has died, it's time to dream another dream. God has so much for you in your future.

If you've settled in any area of your life, take that first step by lifting your eyes to the Father. Let Him renew your strength. Let Him make things new in your life.

A Prayer for Today

Father in Heaven, I lift my eyes up to You and ask You to renew my strength. I praise You for this new day and new season in my life. Thank You for the opportunity to begin again. I refuse to settle for anything less than Your best. I choose to press forward and to keep believing for the dreams and desires You've placed in my heart. I declare You are making all things new! I trust You today with everything that I am in Jesus' Name. Amen.

Wake-Up Thought

Inside each of us there are two people. One says, "I will become everything God has created me to be. I can do all things through Christ. I'm surrounded by God's favor." The other says, "I'll never get out of debt. I'll never lose the weight. I'll never break that addiction. I'll just learn to live with it." One wants to stretch. The other wants to settle. You choose which person you will be.

The Place of Blessing

Today's Scripture

> *Then the word of the LORD came to Elijah: "Leave here, turn eastward and hide in the Kerith Ravine, east of the Jordan. You will drink from the brook, and I have directed the ravens to supply you with food there."*

1 KINGS 17:2–4 NIV

In Scripture, God had a place of provision for Elijah. He gave specific instructions, and as long as Elijah obeyed, he would walk right into His place of blessing.

Just as God directed Elijah to his place of blessing, God is directing you, too. He's aligning the right opportunities for you and causing the right people to come along your path to help you get ahead. He's constantly working behind the scenes on your behalf. But you have to do your part to keep your heart in the right place by following His Word.

That means living in peace and unity. The Bible says that when we live in unity with other believers, there He has commanded the blessing. And when your heart is in the place of blessing, the rest of your life will be in the place of blessing, too!

A Prayer for Today

Father, I love You and come to You with a grateful heart. Thank You for leading me, directing my steps, and pouring out Your blessing upon my life. I declare You are lining up the right opportunities and causing the right people to come along my path! Help me to see others the way You see them so I can live in unity and honor You all the days of my life in Jesus' Name. Amen.

Wake-Up Thought

The great thing is, you don't have to go after blessings; just go after God. Keep Him in first place. Live a life of excellence and integrity, and God promises the blessings will find their way into your hands. This is what Jesus said: "Seek first the kingdom and all these things will be added unto you." Everything you need to fulfill your destiny has already been laid up for you. Just make pleasing God your highest priority.

Letting It Go

Today's Scripture

> *And whenever you stand praying, if you have anything against anyone, forgive him and let it drop (leave it, let it go), in order that your Father Who is in heaven may also forgive you your [own] failings and shortcomings and let them drop.*
>
> MARK 11:25 AMPC

Everyone has been hurt, offended, betrayed, and mistreated at some point. Sometimes those wounds are small and easy to move past, but other times they are deep and take time to heal. The important thing is that we choose to forgive so that we can open the door to God's forgiveness and healing in our own lives.

Forgiveness is such a powerful tool. Forgiveness sets you free and draws you closer to your Heavenly Father. One of the first things my mother did when she found out she had stage four cancer of the liver was to ask the Lord to search her heart for any unforgiveness. She didn't want anything to block her prayers from God's healing. And now more than thirty years later, she still has a perfectly clean bill of health.

Whenever you pray, invite the Lord to search your heart. Choose to forgive anyone who has hurt you. As you walk in forgiveness, you'll experience His hand of blessing in ways you never thought possible, and you will move forward in the abundant life He has in store for you.

A Prayer for Today

Father in Heaven, I worship You and praise You for forgiving me and setting me free. I invite You to search my heart and mind. My desire is to please You and let go of all anger, hurt, and bitterness. I choose forgiveness so that I can receive Your forgiveness in return. I declare that I am moving forward in the abundant life in store for me in Jesus' Name. Amen.

Wake-Up Thought

Being cheated in a business deal, betrayed by a friend, walked out on by a loved one— you may have issues to deal with or people you need to forgive. You can ignore what you know to be true and keep allowing it to poison you and those around you. Or you can make a much better choice by getting it out in the open and asking God to help you totally forgive and let it all go.

Out of the Pit

Today's Scripture

> He lifted me out of the pit of despair, out of the mud and mire. He set my feet on the solid ground and steadied me as I walked along.
>
> PSALM 40:2 NLT

Everyone goes through seasons when they feel as though they are in a pit. That pit can be a frustration or disappointment or a feeling of discouragement, despair, or hopelessness. And maybe you can't see a way out, but you have to know that God is still with you, and He will make a way where there seems to be no way.

Remember, God will never waste anything you go through in life. If you'll keep the right attitude, He'll turn that situation around for your good. It doesn't matter how you got there, whether it was by your own poor choices or maybe someone else treated you unfairly—God wants to use that situation to do a work in you. He'll take that evil and turn it around for your good. You may be uncomfortable at times, but you have to know that you are growing, and God is building your character.

Today, make the decision to shake off any negative, self-defeating mindsets. Choose to cooperate with God. Trust that He is preparing you for promotion. As you keep an attitude of faith, expectancy, and thanksgiving, He will lift you up and set you on the solid path of victory He has in store for you!

A Prayer for Today

Father, today I lift my eyes to You, for my help comes from You. Thank You for doing a work in my life. I choose to cooperate with You and keep an attitude of faith. I believe You are using every situation in my life for my good. I declare You are preparing me for promotion! I praise You today no matter what is going on around me, knowing that You have a good plan for me in Jesus' Name. Amen.

Wake-Up Thought

We all face disappointments, setbacks, unfair situations. At times you may feel as though you've been thrown into a pit. But instead of being discouraged and letting it cloud your vision, just look inside yourself. You will see that the pit does not match up with the vision God put in your heart. You can say: "This is not permanent. This is just another stop on the way to my divine destiny!"

Do Good

Today's Scripture

> ...even Jesus of Nazareth, how God anointed him with the Holy Spirit and with power; who went about doing good, and healing all that were oppressed of the devil; for God was with him.
>
> ACTS 10:38 ASV

The first thing Jesus did before healing, before ministering, before delivering is that He was good to people. Think about that for a moment. We all have an assignment. You could say that we all have a ministry. It may not be up in front of people. It may not be to go overseas and be a missionary. Our ministry starts by being good to people.

When goodness flows out of our hearts, it catches people's attention. It causes them to want to know more about what we have. We can say all day long, "I love you," but true love is seen in what we do. If I really love you, I'll be good to you. I'll prefer you. God said to Abraham, "I will bless you, and you will be a blessing." One key to being blessed is: are you willing to be a blessing? Are you willing to do good?

A Prayer for Today

Father God, I love You and praise You for all You have done in my life. Today I ask that You empower me to do good. Help me to be more aware of the people and needs around me. My desire is to love others as You have loved me. Use me to be a blessing and a testimony of Your goodness so that others may come to know You in Jesus' Name. Amen.

Wake-Up Thought

This morning, look around at who's in your life. Listen to what they're saying. You can't help everyone, but you can help someone. There are people whom God has put in your path who are connected to your destiny. You can lift the fallen. You can restore the broken. You can be kind to a stranger. As you help them rise higher, you will rise higher. As you meet their needs, God will meet your needs.

Bring Forth the Treasures

Today's Scripture

> "A good man brings good things out of the good stored up in him."

MATTHEW 12:35 NIV

Recently, there was an article that told how the wealthiest places on earth are not the oil fields of the Middle East or the diamond mines of South Africa. The wealthiest places are the cemeteries. Buried in the ground are businesses that were never formed, songs that were never composed, books that were never written, potential that was never realized, and dreams that never came to pass.

Don't let that be you! Don't go to your grave with your treasure still in you. Keep growing. Keep learning. Step out in faith and trust God. Bring forth the good treasure that God has placed within you. If you don't know where to start, start by meditating on His Word. Let Him speak to your heart. Learn to hear His voice. Learn to obey quickly. Trust that He is good and will lead you in the path He has prepared for you.

A Prayer for Today

Father, thank You for the good treasures that You've deposited in me. I will stir up the gifts You have given me and I will be faithful to develop what You've entrusted to me. I declare I will reach my full potential! Help me, by Your Holy Spirit, to stay close to You and follow Your leading every step of the way in Jesus' Name. Amen.

Wake-Up Thought

You have to be proactive and take these steps to grow. You should be doing something intentional and strategic every day to improve your skills. Don't be vague in your approach. Do not say things such as: "If I have time, I'll do it." You are better than that. You have too much in you to stay where you are. Your destiny is too great to hold back.

Get Ready for the New

Today's Scripture

> *"See, I am doing a new thing! Now it springs up; do you not perceive it? I am making a way in the wilderness and streams in the wasteland."*
>
> Isaiah 43:19 niv

Are you ready for a new chapter in your life? Sometimes, in order to move forward into the blessing God has for you, you have to be willing to let go of the old. The things that are behind you are not nearly as important as what is out in front of you. It's time to get ready for the new!

You may have had some unfair things happen, things that you don't understand; but let me tell you, you have come too far to stop now. Instead of allowing those things to hold you back, why don't you let go and take a step of faith into the new? It's time to get a new, bigger vision; it's time to get a new, fresher outlook; it's time to rise up with a new attitude! Instead of settling where you are, pick up and move forward. Have the attitude that says, *I may not understand it; it may not have been fair, but I am not getting stuck on this page. I know God has a new chapter for me—a chapter filled with blessings, favor, and victory!*

A Prayer for Today

Father, thank You for Your faithfulness in my life. Today I choose to trust You with my past, present, and future. I am making the decision to move forward from this moment on. Give me wisdom to discern the seasons of my life and teach me to embrace the new things You have in store for me. I declare You have a new chapter for me filled with blessings, favor, and victory in Jesus' Name! Amen.

Wake-Up Thought

If you could write your best life story this morning, what would it say? Is your first reaction to see and describe yourself in terms of past experiences or present limitations, more in terms of losing or just surviving rather than fulfilling your dreams? If you've packed away your dreams, dare to unpack them today and ask God to rekindle them in your heart and mind. It's time to enlarge your vision.

Hope

I pray that God, the source of hope, will fill you completely with joy and peace because you trust in him. Then you will overflow with confident hope through the power of the Holy Spirit.

ROMANS 15:13 NLT

Remain Confident of This

Today's Scripture

> *I remain confident of this: I will see the goodness of the* LORD *in the land of the living.*
>
> PSALM 27:13 NIV

When David wrote Psalm 27, he was going through a tough time. Things weren't going his way. But he said in effect, "I'm not worried. I'm not upset. I am confident that I will see God's goodness." In other words, "This situation I'm in may be rough, but that's not going to steal my vision. That's not going to cause me to give up on my dreams. I am confident that I will see God's favor in a new way."

That's what your attitude needs to be today, because what you focus on is what you will see. No matter what the medical report says, no matter what your finances look like, no matter how bad that relationship may seem, be confident that you will see His goodness! He is the all-powerful, omniscient, Creator of the universe, and He holds you in the palm of His hand. Nothing is too difficult for Him. Take hold of this truth by faith and focus on His goodness today. Allow His peace to settle in your heart and mind as you move forward in His blessing all the days of your life!

A Prayer for Today

Father, thank You for Your goodness in my life and that You hold me in the palm of Your hand. I choose to set my heart and mind on You today  *no matter what my circumstances may look like. I will focus on Your promises. I am confident that I will see Your goodness! Give me Your peace as I keep my mind fixed on You in Jesus' Name. Amen.*

Wake-Up Thought

What are you expecting in life? Are you anticipating good things or bad things, significance or mediocrity? Don't allow your circumstances or feelings to dull your enthusiasm for life and imprison you in a negative frame of mind. Starting today, expect to experience the goodness of God! If you will live with an attitude of faith, before long God's goodness is going to show up, and that difficult situation will turn around to your benefit.

Getting Quiet

Today's Scripture

Be still, and know that I am God.

PSALM 46:10 NKJV

So many people today find themselves caught up in the day-to-day busyness of life, driven to do more in less time. It seems people constantly strive to find ways to cram more into their already overcrowded schedules. But at the same time, God is constantly inviting us to step away from the hectic pace of life and come to Him to find rest for our souls. He invites us to be still before Him, to get quiet so we can hear His voice and set our hearts and minds at peace.

Every day, you should take time to read the Scripture and meditate on God's promises. Every time you're in the car, put on some good praise music. Make it a point to spend time with God throughout the day. When you get quiet, say, "God, I love You today. Lord, thank

You for my life, my family, my dreams." That's what is going to keep you strong. That's what's going to keep you moving forward in the right direction.

Today, make it a point to be still before God. Quiet your mind of all the things on your agenda and just focus on Him. Let Him love you, let Him speak to your heart, and let Him fill you with peace and strength each and every day.

A Prayer for Today

Father, thank You for Your love and grace that are upon me. Right now, I let go of all the distractions of life and focus on You. I choose to be still, to get quiet before You, and listen to You. Restore me and help me to hear Your voice with clarity. I receive Your peace and strength for today in Jesus' Name. Amen.

Wake-Up Thought

The Scripture says that in God's presence there is fullness of joy, fullness of peace, fullness of victory. That's where you're refreshed and restored. Take time at the beginning of each day to sit quietly in His presence, pray, and read your Bible. When you get alone with God and put Him first, the rest of your day will go much better. You will reap rich rewards and live the abundant life He has for you.

He Opens and Closes Doors

Today's Scripture

> *"I know your works. Behold, I have set before you an open door, which no one is able to shut. I know that you have but little power, and yet you have kept my word and have not denied my name."*
>
> REVELATION 3:8 ESV

God opens doors of opportunity before us that no one is able to shut. But we have to realize, sometimes He also closes doors because He has something better in store. We may see a logical opportunity, but just because it's the logical way doesn't mean that it's God's way. Just because it happened that way before doesn't mean it's going to happen that way next time. That's why you have to stay open and keep trusting in God. If you're narrow-minded and only look at the door that's been closed, you may miss the door He has opened behind you!

When you are able to let go of your own agenda and trust God, He'll make sure you see those open doors. Scripture says His Word is what lights our path. Our attitude should always be, *God, I surrender all to You. Have Your way in my life. I trust Your timing. God, I trust You to do it Your way.* Then step back and see the open door that He has prepared for you!

A Prayer for Today

Father, I praise You today and thank You for ordering and directing my steps. I choose to trust You even when doors close before me. I believe that You have my best interest at heart. I am ready and available. I surrender all to You. I stand looking for the open doors You have for me. Help me to be sensitive to Your leading in Jesus' Name. Amen.

Wake-Up Thought

Too many people, because they've hit several closed doors in a row, lose their passion. You may have been turned down, delayed, overlooked. That was all a part of God's plan. Now here's the key: you have to go through your closed doors before you reach your open doors. When you come to a closed door, instead of being discouraged, the correct attitude is, I'm one step closer to my open door.

When You Pray

Today's Scripture

> *"And whenever you stand praying, if you have anything against anyone, forgive him, that your Father in heaven may also forgive you your trespasses."*
>
> MARK 11:25 NKJV

Many times people wonder why their prayers aren't answered. They feel distant from God but can't explain why. They love God and try to do all the right things, but deep inside they sense that something isn't right.

Scripture tells us there are many things that can hinder our prayers. One of them is unforgiveness. God knows that holding unforgiveness is destructive because it puts up a wall between us and Him. But when we choose to forgive, the wall comes down. Someone said it like this: "Forgiveness is setting the prisoner free and realizing the prisoner was you."

When you go before God in prayer, ask Him to search your heart and mind. See if there is any unforgiveness that is blocking your prayers and affecting your relationship with Him. The other person may have been wrong, they may have hurt you deeply, but there is nothing on this earth that is worth losing your peace with Almighty God. Forgiveness doesn't excuse the other person; it means you are trusting God with it all. Today, when you pray, choose forgiveness and don't let anything stand in the way of the good things God has in store for your future!

A Prayer for Today

Father, I love You and I humbly come to You today with an open and willing heart. Search me. Know me. Show me if there is any unforgiveness in my life or anything that would displease You. Thank You for showing me Your ways so I can walk with You in peace all the days of my life in Jesus' Name. Amen.

Wake-Up Thought

You can have success on the outside, but if you have unforgiveness and bitterness on the inside, it's going to spoil and taint every victory. We attempt to cram unforgiveness, resentment, and anger into our "leakproof" containers, but one day the things you have tamped into your subconscious or buried deeply in the recesses of your heart will rise to the surface. Forgiveness is the key to being free from toxic bitterness.

Yoke Destroyer

Today's Scripture

> *And it shall come to pass in that day, that his burden shall be taken away from off thy shoulder, and his yoke from off thy neck, and the yoke shall be destroyed because of the anointing.*
>
> ISAIAH 10:27 KJV

A yoke is something that is put around the neck of an ox to help control the animal. It limits its movement. If the ox starts to get off course, the yoke is used to pull it back. Even though an ox is very powerful, this small yoke keeps it from doing what it wants to do.

Some people don't realize today that they're living with a yoke around their neck. They wonder why they can't get ahead or why everything is a struggle. It's because of the yokes that are dragging them down. Negative words that were spoken over you can become a yoke. Every time you start to step out, you hear the voice of a parent or a coach saying, "You're not that talented; you don't have what it takes." It plays again and again. Eventually, you shrink back. That's a yoke.

Today, know that God's burden-moving, yoke-destroying power will set you free! Call on Him and let Him set you free from every bondage of the past. Choose to forgive and release the yoke of bitterness. Don't go around being burdened any longer. Study His Word and let His anointing set you free to live in total victory!

A Prayer for Today

Father God, I love You and give You all the glory. Thank You for destroying every yoke of bondage off of my life. I choose to surrender every hurt and pain of the past to You. I choose to live by Your Word, which is life to my soul. Thank You for Your anointing at work in my life to destroy every yoke and set me free. I declare that whom the Son sets free is free indeed in Jesus' Name! Amen.

Wake-Up Thought

Jesus said, "My yoke is easy and My burden is light." God's favor and blessing on your life are lightening the load and taking the pressure off. He has already lined up solutions to your problems. What used to be difficult will not be difficult anymore. You will get breaks that you didn't deserve. You will have good ideas, wisdom, creativity, and you won't know where it came from. This is God's anointing of ease on your life.

Heaven's Currency

Today's Scripture

> *And whatever you ask for in prayer, having faith and [really] believing, you will receive.*
>
> MATTHEW 21:22 AMPC

In the natural realm, we exchange money for the things we want and need. But in the spiritual realm, faith is what we exchange. The Bible tells us that when you pray with faith, you will receive it. Faith moves mountains. Faith pleases God. Faith is what opens spiritual doors. What is faith? It's believing in God and His goodness. It's knowing that He is a rewarder of those who diligently seek Him. Faith is believing that the promises of God are true. It's obeying His Word. Faith causes you to act.

Where does faith come from? It's a gift from God. Everyone is given a measure of faith, but we have to be a good steward of it and help it grow. Romans tell us that faith grows by hearing the Word of God. The more you hear the Word of God, the more your faith will grow. The more your faith grows, the more you will see the promises of God come to pass in every area of your life. Remember, faith is Heaven's currency. So invest your faith by investing time in His Word.

A Prayer for Today

Father in Heaven, thank You for Your loving-kindness and tender mercies. Thank You for giving me a measure of faith and the gift of Your Word that is a light to my path and a lamp to my feet. Help me grow in the knowledge of You and Your Word. Give me the spirit of wisdom and revelation. I declare I am getting stronger spiritually and in every area! I choose to set my heart and mind on Your Word and listen as You speak Your truth to my heart in Jesus' Name. Amen!

Wake-Up Thought

In life, there are always two voices competing for your attention—the voice of faith and the voice of defeat. You'll hear a voice piping in, "The problem is insurmountable. It's not going to work out." But if you listen carefully, the voice of faith is saying, "God has a way. Breakthroughs are coming." The other voice may seem louder, but you can override it. You can take away all of its power by choosing to listen to the voice of faith.

He Restores Your Soul

Today's Scripture

> The LORD is my shepherd; I shall
> not be in want. He makes me to
> lie down in green pastures; He
> leads me beside the still waters. He
> restores my soul.
>
> PSALM 23:1–3 NKJV

God wants to restore your soul. What does that mean? Your soul is your mind, will, and emotions. You are a three-part being: you have a spirit, which is the part of you that lives for eternity, you have a soul, and you live in a body while you're here on earth.

Your soul is where the enemy tries to attack you and hold you back. Your soul is where you may have brokenness from the past or hurts and disappointments, but when God restores your soul, He brings His healing power to those broken places. He makes you whole again. And when God restores you, He makes you better off than you were before!

Notice that He leads us beside quiet waters. He makes us lie down in green pastures. This is a picture of rest. When we are resting in Him, He is able to do a work in our lives. He is able to bring that restoration. Don't let the busyness of life keep you going so fast that you don't stop and rest. Take time to be still before the Lord and meditate on His Word. Let Him restore and heal your soul so that you can embrace all the good things He has in store for you!

A Prayer for Today

Father, thank You for another day to praise You. Thank You for being my good Shepherd and for leading me into the place of rest. I ask You to restore my soul. Renew my joy. Heal my heart as I surrender every area of my life to You. I expect my future to be bright because You are restoring my soul. I declare I am healed and whole in Jesus' Name. Amen.

Wake-Up Thought

No matter what you've been through, no matter whose fault it was, God wants to turn it around and restore everything that has been stolen from you. He wants to restore your marriage, your family, your career. He wants to restore those broken dreams. He wants to restore your joy and give you a peace and happiness you've never known before. Most of all, He wants to restore your relationship with Him. God wants you to live a satisfied life.

Set the Tone

Today's Scripture

> I will praise the LORD at all times.
> I will constantly speak his praises.
>
> PSALM 34:1 NLT

When you wake up in the morning, what's the first thing you think about? What's the first thing you say? Do you set the tone for success, favor, and blessing?

Yesterday may have had some hardships or some difficulties, but it's a new day. We should be on the lookout for God's blessings.

The Scripture tells us that the darker it gets in the world, the brighter it's going to be for God's people. The path of the righteous is like the light of dawn shining brighter until the new day. Things may be bad all around you, people may be negative, complaining and discouraged, but don't let that rub off on you.

The worse it gets, the brighter you're going to shine. Be determined to set the tone for your day by praising God and speaking words of faith over your future. Be determined to shine. Stand strong in faith and set the tone for your future!

A Prayer for Today

Father in Heaven, I love You and worship You. Thank You for Your goodness in my life. You are good and Your mercy endures forever. I choose to start my day with You and set the tone for my day and future. I receive Your favor, grace, mercy, wisdom, and strength. Help me to receive all You have for me. Thank You for Your faithfulness to me at all times in Jesus' Name! Amen!

Wake-Up Thought

Every morning when you wake up, you should declare, "Something good is going to happen to me today." You have to set the tone at the beginning of each day. Then all through the day you should have this attitude of expectancy. Your expectation is your faith at work. When you expect good breaks, expect people to like you, or expect to have a great year, you're releasing your faith. That's what allows good things to happen.

Get Your Joy Back

Today's Scripture

> *Though you have not seen him,*
> *you love him; and even though*
> *you do not see him now, you*
> *believe in him and are filled with*
> *an inexpressible and glorious joy.*
>
> 1 PETER 1:8 NIV

If the circumstances of life have taken away your joy, today is the day to get it back. You weren't meant to live this life feeling drained, depressed, and down. God wants you to be excited about your future and learn to enjoy each and every day.

If you don't make the conscious effort to keep your joy, year after year you'll get more and more solemn. Not only will the enemy rob you of the joy that belongs to you, but he'll rob your family and friends of the gift that you have to give them. When you have joy, you can use that joy to influence the people around you for good. Joy is strength, and when you have joy, you can offer strength to the people God has placed in your life.

Today, draw the line in the sand and say, "That's it. I'm not going to live another day negative, discouraged, sour, and grumpy. I'm going to put a smile on my face. I'm going to live my life happy." Choose to hold on to joy, which is your strength, so you can offer strength to people everywhere you go.

A Prayer for Today

*Father in Heaven, I praise You and thank
You that the joy of the Lord is my strength.
I choose to put a smile on my face and live
a joy-filled life. Today, help me to spread joy
everywhere I go. I am blessed to be a blessing
and I invite You to fill me with Your
inexpressible, glorious joy so that I can be a
blessing to the people You have placed in my
life in Jesus' Name. Amen.*

Wake-Up Thought

*The Bible says that "the joy of the
Lord is your strength." Your enemy
knows that if he can deceive you
into living down in the dumps and
depressed, you are not going to have
the necessary strength—physically,
emotionally, or spiritually—
to withstand his attacks. Keep
giving God praise despite your
circumstances, and you will enjoy your life
to the fullest today.*

Answer the Door

Today's Scripture

> *Weeping may last through the night, but joy comes with the morning.*
>
> PSALM 30:5 NLT

S cripture says that joy comes in the morning. When you wake up each morning, God sends you a special delivery of joy. It comes knocking at your door. When you get up in faith and make the declaration that "this is going to be a good day," do you know what you just did? You just answered the door. You just received the gift of joy that God sent to you. The problem is that some people never answer the door.

Joy has been knocking for months and months, years and years, saying, "Come on! Let me in! You can be happy! You can cheer up! You can enjoy your life!"

Why don't you make up your mind to answer the door for joy! Decide to wake up every morning and say, "Father, thank You for another beautiful day. I'm going to be happy. I'm going to enjoy this day. I'm going to brighten somebody else's life. I am choosing to answer the door and receive Your gift of joy today!"

A Prayer for Today

Father, I praise You for another beautiful day. Your mercies toward me are new every morning. Thank You for giving me joy and supernatural peace. Thank You for walking me through the difficult times of life. No matter what I am going through, I will not let anyone or anything steal my joy. I choose to answer the door for joy every single morning so that I can walk in the strength You have given to me in Jesus' Name. Amen.

Wake-Up Thought

Expect to open the door to joy. If you raise your level of joy expectancy, God will take you places you've never dreamed. Expect breakthroughs. Expect problems to turn around. Expect to rise to new levels. You haven't seen your greatest victories. You haven't accomplished your greatest dreams. God will help you overcome obstacles that looked insurmountable, and you will see His goodness in amazing ways.

With Your Whole Heart

Today's Scripture

> Whatever your hand finds to
> do, do it with all your might.
>
> ECCLESIASTES 9:10 NIV

When you do something to the best of your ability because you want to honor God, it opens the door to His blessing. That means it will be easier, it will go better, and you will accomplish more. That's why no matter what we do, we should give it our best. This is especially true even in the little things. For example, when you're doing the dishes or mowing the lawn, don't drag around sour and frustrated. Mow with enthusiasm! Mow like you're on a mission from God. With every step, thank God that your legs work. Thank Him that you're healthy and strong.

At the office, don't just do enough to get by. You're not working unto people; you're working unto God. Do it with your whole heart. When you volunteer at church, don't wake up on Sunday morning and think, *Awe, man. Why did I volunteer? I want to sleep in!* No, serve Him with all your heart because that's what honors God. When you honor God, He will honor you. He will open the door to His blessing, and you'll see increase in every area of your life!

A Prayer for Today

Father, thank You for Your hand of blessing on my life. Thank You for health and strength and life. I choose to serve You with my whole heart, with enthusiasm, and to do everything to the best of my ability. I declare doors of blessing are opening and increase is coming because I honor You. Thank You for Your faithfulness and goodness in my life in Jesus' Name. Amen.

Wake-Up Thought

Don't drag through the day. Don't get stuck in a rut. Whatever you do, put your heart into it. You are sowing a seed when you go to work with a smile, put a spring in your step, give it your best, offer kindness to others, and show gratitude for what you have. You honor God when you do it with all your heart, and He will take that seed and grow it to bring something exciting into your life.

Good Medicine

Today's Scripture

> *A joyful heart is good medicine, but a crushed spirit dries up the bones.*

PROVERBS 17:22 ESV

Throughout life, there will always be something that will try to take our joy. If it's not a grumpy salesperson, it's a family member aggravating you, traffic is backed up, your flight is delayed, or your spouse is taking too long. Don't go the next twenty years allowing the same people and the same circumstances to frustrate you. Change your approach. What's upsetting you now doesn't have to upset you anymore.

You can choose to keep your cool and stay calm and steady. Remember, a relaxed attitude is going to lengthen your life. The next time you're tempted to be upset, ask yourself, "Is this really worth giving up my joy over?"

If you'll make this decision not to give away your joy but to live each day happy, God promises you'll be strong, you'll have more peaceful relationships, and you'll accomplish more. He says a joyful heart is good medicine! Hold on to your joy and let it heal your heart so you can experience the blessings He has in store for you!

A Prayer for Today

Father in Heaven, I love You and honor You. Today I will hold on to joy! I am not going to live my life upset. I choose to live each day with peace and happiness, serving You with my whole heart. I choose to rely on Your strength and Your Word that guides my every step. Help me to spread joy, encouragement, and enthusiasm everywhere I go in Jesus' Name. Amen.

Wake-Up Thought

Some people have lost their joy because they are dragging around all this baggage from the past. They have their bags full of resentment, guilt and condemnation, disappointment, regrets, and bitterness. Life is too short to live that way. At the start of the day, let go of the setbacks and the disappointments from yesterday. Start every morning afresh and anew and let the joy in.

Overcome with Good

Today's Scripture

> *Do not be overcome by evil,*
> *but overcome evil with good.*

ROMANS 12:21 NIV

The Scripture says, "We overcome evil with good." In other words, when somebody's rude or inconsiderate, don't sink to their level. Don't be rude and inconsiderate back to them. No, if you are going to rise higher, if you are going to overcome, you have to do just the opposite. You have to show kindness, grace, and mercy. It isn't always easy; in fact, it's almost never easy. It takes a lot of humility to treat someone with respect who is disrespecting you. But do you know what happens when you walk in humility? God gives you His grace. He empowers you to walk in His goodness. Scripture plainly says,

"God opposes the proud but gives grace to the humble."

Today, show mercy and sow mercy. Receive His grace, receive His power, and receive His strength to be everything He's called you to be.

A Prayer for Today

Father God, I love You and give You all the praise and glory. Thank You for giving me the grace to overcome in this life. I choose to overcome evil with good by the help of the Holy Spirit. Help me to show love and mercy and sow love and mercy. I desire to walk in peace and humility in every circumstance in Jesus' Name. Amen.

Wake-Up Thought

If you mistreat people who are mistreating you, you will make matters worse. When you express anger to somebody who has been angry with you, it's like adding fuel to a fire. No, you overcome evil with good. When somebody hurts you, the only way you can overcome it is by showing them mercy, forgiving them, and doing what is right. Remain calm and peaceable even when those around you are not.

A Different Spirit

Today's Scripture

> "But My servant Caleb, because
> he has had a different spirit and
> has followed Me fully, I will bring
> into the land which he entered,
> and his descendants shall take
> possession of it."
>
> NUMBERS 14:24 NASB

One time in Scripture, Moses sent twelve men to spy out the Promised Land. The people of Israel were camped right next door and excited about possessing the land. But after forty days, ten of the men came back with a negative report. They said, "Moses, there are giants in the land, and we'll never defeat them." That negative report spread throughout the rest of the camp, and the people began to murmur and complain. But one of the spies named Caleb said, "Moses, we are well able to defeat these people. Let us go up at once and take the land!"

It's interesting that they all saw the same land and the same circumstances, yet they had totally different views. How could their reports be so opposite? Here's how: Caleb had a different spirit. He saw things with a different perspective. Others were focused on the giants, but Caleb was focused on his God. The people who complained never actually made it into the Promised Land, but Caleb did. He accompanied a new generation that chose the blessing of God.

Today, you can choose to have a different spirit. Don't listen to what everyone else says; listen to what God says. Choose to believe His Word, choose to obey Him, and He will lead you into your promised land!

A Prayer for Today

Father, thank You for Your goodness in my life. Today I choose to tune out the negative voices of the world. I choose to trust in You even when no one else around me will. Help me to have a spirit of faith and courage. I thank You for the good things You are doing in my life and trust that You will fulfill every promise You've made to me in Jesus' Name. Amen.

Wake-Up Thought

If you were among the twelve Hebrew spies sent by Moses into Canaan to check out the opposition, what report would you deliver this morning? Caleb saw giants in the Promised Land, believed God, and refused to see himself as a grasshopper as the other ten spies saw themselves. Instead, he saw himself as God's man, led and empowered by God. What a tremendous truth! See yourself as God sees you, and start seeing yourself as winning.

Nothing Wasted

Today's Scripture

> *When they had all had enough to eat, he said to his disciples, "Gather the pieces that are left over. Let nothing be wasted."*
>
> JOHN 6:12 NIV

The Bible tells of a time when Jesus fed a crowd of five thousand with only five loaves and two fishes. He blessed it and multiplied it. That day, everyone had more than enough to eat, and there were still twelve baskets full of bread and fish left over. That's because we serve a God of abundance! Then Jesus told the disciples to collect all the leftovers "so that nothing is wasted." With God, nothing is ever wasted. He'll never waste an experience; He'll never waste a hurt; He'll never waste a dream; He'll never waste even a single piece of bread.

If you've felt as though you've wasted years of your life in the wrong job, hanging around the wrong people, or doing the wrong things, God will gather those years and restore them to you. He'll take those experiences that the enemy meant for your harm and turn them around for your good. He'll make you stronger, wiser, and better off than you were before. He can launch you further into your destiny than before. Be encouraged today because with God, all things are possible! He is your provider, and nothing is ever wasted!

A Prayer for Today

Father, I love You and appreciate all You have done for me. I give You every bit of my life—my past, my present, and my future. Thank You that You are a God of restoration. I trust You to take every negative experience and turn it around for my good. I know that with You nothing is ever wasted in Jesus' Name! Amen.

Wake-Up Thought

You may have had some setbacks or disappointments, or you tried something that didn't work out. These were not a waste of your time. Every challenge you've gone through has deposited something on the inside of you. God doesn't waste anything. You are not defined by your past. You are prepared by your past. You're on the runway about to take off.

Attitude in Adversity

Today's Scripture

Let this same attitude and purpose and [humble] mind be in you which was in Christ Jesus.

PHILIPPIANS 2:5 AMPC

There's an old saying, "Attitude determines altitude." In other words, a positive, faith-filled attitude will cause you to rise higher in life, but a negative, self-critical attitude will only drag you down.

When we face adversity, our attitude affects the outcome. Are we going to treat people right even when we're being mistreated? Are we going to stay full of joy even when the bottom falls out? So many people get all bent out of shape and start complaining when things don't go their way, but that kind of attitude only closes the door to God's miracle-working power. The Bible says that faith is what pleases

God. Understand that He's trying to work in your life. He's trying to get you prepared for promotion, but you have to stay on His side. You have to stand strong and fight that good fight of faith!

If you are going through a difficult time, keep an attitude of faith and expectancy. Start thanking God for bringing you through to the other side. As you stand strong, believe you'll come out stronger and wiser, and you will continue moving forward in the abundant life God has for you!

A Prayer for Today

Heavenly Father, thank You for Your unconditional love and mercy. Today I choose to have a positive, faith-filled attitude. I choose to worship You and trust You even when things don't make sense in my natural mind. I know You have a good plan for me and that You are working all things out for my good in Jesus' Name. Amen.

Wake-Up Thought

God works where there is an attitude of faith. Dwell on the fact that Almighty God is on your side. Stand on the fact that He's promised to fight your battles for you. Dwell on the truth that no weapon formed against you can prosper. If you start thinking these kinds of thoughts, you will be filled with faith and confidence, no matter what comes against you today.

Look Beneath the Surface

Today's Scripture

> *"Look beneath the surface so you can judge correctly."*
>
> JOHN 7:24 NLT

You may have heard that it takes six seconds to make a first impression. Most people don't realize how many times they look at someone and instantly decide if they're going to like them or not. The Scripture says that man looks at the outward appearance of others while God looks at the heart. Now you might be thinking, *Of course, God looks at the heart. He's God. How am I supposed to look at another person's heart?* You may not exactly know a person's heart, but as Jesus said in this verse, you can look beneath the surface. You can take time to get to know someone who might look or act differently than you. Don't just write someone off because they don't measure up to your standard. You never know how God will use that relationship in your life.

Jesus said, "Whatever you've done to the least of these, you've done to Me." In other words, when we make quick judgments about people, it's as if we are making quick judgments about God. Don't fall into that trap! Instead, look beneath the surface. Look for the good in others, find some common ground, and watch what God will do through the relationships in your life!

A Prayer for Today

Father in Heaven, I praise and worship You with all my heart. Thank You for seeing the best in me and overlooking my faults. Help me to look beneath the surface and see the value in people. I want to see others through Your eyes. Show me how to connect with others and be a blessing everywhere I go in Jesus' Name. Amen.

Wake-Up Thought

True religion doesn't judge people to see if they deserve our help. Jesus said, "It's the sick who need the doctor, not the healthy." God didn't call us to judge people; He called us to heal people. He called us to restore people. When you get down low to lift somebody up, in God's eyes, you can't get any higher. The closest thing to the heart of God is helping hurting people.

JOEL & VICTORIA OSTEEN

Like a Flood

Today's Scripture

> *When the enemy shall come in like a flood, the Spirit of the LORD shall lift up a standard against him.*
>
> ISAIAH 59:19 KJV

We all have times when we feel overwhelmed by life. You get a bad report, unexpected news, or someone you trusted wrongs you. What does God do? He doesn't sit back and think, *Too bad. Sorry your life is so difficult.* No, when the enemy comes in like a flood, God raises up a barrier. In other words, that injustice, that bad break, that sickness gets God's attention. He doesn't sit back. He goes to work!

It's like a parent with a child. If someone or something is giving them a hard time, you don't think twice. You stop what you're doing and immediately go to help. That's the way it is with our Heavenly Father. When the enemy comes in like a flood, God steps up and says, "Hey, wait a minute. You're messing with the wrong person! That's My son. That's My daughter. If you're going to mess with them, you're going to have to first mess with Me—the all-powerful Creator of the universe."

You have to realize that in the tough times, you're not alone. You have somebody fighting for you. The Most High God has your back.

A Prayer for Today

Father, I praise You for Your hand of protection upon my life. I thank You for being my Heavenly Father and watching over me. I choose to stand strong in faith, knowing that You are fighting my battles for me and working behind the scenes on my behalf. Even when the enemy comes in like a flood, You are raising up a standard for me in Jesus' Name! Amen.

Wake-Up Thought

You may be in what feels like a raging flood today. There may be pressure all around you. Maybe you can't see the end. You could easily be worried, but know this: the battle is not yours. The battle is the Lord's. God is saying, "If you'll trust Me, I will lift up a standard against the enemy, and instead of the flood destroying you, I will use it to thrust you forward."

Be Still and Know

Today's Scripture

> He says, "Be still, and know that I am God."
>
> PSALM 46:10 NIV

In our world today, most people are used to having constant activity: computers, cell phones, television, email, video games. There's nothing wrong with any of that, but the Bible tells us that we need to stop and be still so we can focus on knowing God. This is especially true during the difficult times. When you are facing a challenge, it's easy to want to run to a friend or talk about it with a coworker. But at some point, you have to stop and say, "God, I rest in You. I know You have me in the palm of Your hand."

Remember, our battles are spiritual battles. The people in your life aren't the source of your problems; the forces of darkness are. When you choose to be still and know that the Creator of the universe lives on the inside of you, you are putting yourself in a position of strength. So today, take time to be still before Him. Let His peace cover you. Let Him refresh you by His Spirit. Remember, the battles you face belong to the Lord. Be still before Him so you can see His hand of victory in every area of your life!

A Prayer for Today

Father in Heaven, I love You and worship You. I humbly come before You to learn from You and listen to You. I choose to be still in Your presence. Speak to my heart so I can know You more. I cast my cares upon You because You care for me. Fill me with Your peace as I put my trust in You in Jesus' Name. Amen.

Wake-Up Thought

So often we think we have to do it only in our own strength. When you feel overwhelmed and you're tempted to take everything into your own hands, you have to make yourself be still. God is saying to you, "Be still. I have it all figured out. I control the whole universe. I've already set the time to not only deliver you, but to bring you out better off than you were before."

Hope

"For I know the plans I have for you," declares the LORD, "plans to prosper you and not to harm you, plans to give you hope and a future."

JEREMIAH 29:11 NIV

Ignore the Critics

Today's Scripture

> When Peter went up to
> Jerusalem, the circumcised
> believers criticized him.

ACTS 11:2 NIV

One time, Jesus was in the temple. It was on the Sabbath, their day of rest. He saw a man with a withered hand. Jesus simply said, "Stretch forth your hand," and immediately the man was healed. The religious leaders, the Pharisees, were there and didn't like Jesus. Even though He did something great, they ridiculed Him for doing it on the Sabbath, the day of rest.

No matter what you do, some people are not going to be for you. Even if you changed, met all their demands, and did everything they asked, they would still find something wrong. But we can all save ourselves a lot of heartache and pain by learning to ignore those critical voices. You don't need those people's approval. You don't have to have them cheering you on. They may try to make you look bad, but if you will stay on the high road and let God fight your battles, the more they talk the more God will bless you. They may try to take you down, but God will use it to take you up. Keep focused on your future, keep focused on the Word, and let His truth strengthen you to ignore the critics!

A Prayer for Today

Father, I love You and give You all the praise and glory. Today I set my heart and focus on You. I choose to ignore the critical voices that would try to distract me from Your plan. I declare that no one or nothing can stop Your plans and purposes. Help me to forgive those who come against me and to always walk in love so that I can honor You in Jesus' Name. Amen.

Wake-Up Thought

Everyone has a right to an opinion, and you have every right to not listen to it. If what others say doesn't match what God has put in your heart, let it go. It's fine to listen to opinions, but you have to be secure enough in who God made you to be, that when something doesn't bear witness with your spirit, you'll have a boldness that says, "Thanks. I value your opinion, but that's not for me."

Press Through

Today's Scripture

> Keep on asking and it will be given you; keep on seeking and you will find; keep on knocking [reverently] and [the door] will be opened to you.

MATTHEW 7:7 AMPC

I n Mark, chapter five, there was a woman who had been sick for twelve years. The doctors gave her no hope. But she heard that Jesus was coming through her town. Something deep on the inside said to her, "This is your season. This is your time to get well." In the natural, when she saw all the people around Him, she thought, *I'll never get to Him. It's so crowded and I'm weak. I just don't think I can do this.* She almost missed her season. But instead of dwelling on those negative thoughts, she started reminding herself, *If I can just get to Jesus, I will be whole.* She made the choice to turn her thoughts in the right direction. She kept pressing her way through the crowd until she got just close enough to Jesus to reach out and touch the edge of His robe. Instantly, she was made whole. This is what Jesus said: "Daughter, your faith has made you well."

Notice, it was her faith and her persistence that connected her with God's power, and the same is true for us today. No matter what you are facing, don't give up! Keep praying! Keep asking! Keep seeking! God is faithful! Stay determined because He will meet your faith with His miraculous power when you continue to press through!

A Prayer for Today

Heavenly Father, I come to You today with an open and humble heart. I love You and appreciate You. I ask You to fill me with Your strength, peace, and joy so that I can see my dreams come to pass. I refuse to give up! I declare I am patient, I am persistent, and I will press through to victory! Show me Your miraculous power in Jesus' Name. Amen.

Wake-Up Thought

You may have received a bad report from the doctor, knocking you off your feet and pushing you into the pit. You  *may be in a situation today where you have done your best. You've prayed and placed your faith firmly on the truth of God's Word. But nothing's changed. When you're tempted to say, "What's the use?" God is saying, "Don't cast away your confidence, for payday is coming."*

It's No Surprise to God

Today's Scripture

> *"For I know the plans I have for you," declares the* LORD, *"plans to prosper you and not to harm you, plans to give you hope and a future."*

JEREMIAH 29:11 NIV

I n life, we all experience things that are unexpected. But when something unplanned happens, we have to realize that it's no surprise to God.

Maybe you are dealing with some sort of loss. It hit you unexpectedly. You could be discouraged and overwhelmed and say, "I can't believe this is happening." No, have a new perspective. That situation is no surprise to God. It didn't catch Him off guard. He has already anointed you. You have the strength you need. You have the peace, the determination, the confidence. You're not lacking. You're anointed! The forces that are for you are greater than the forces that are against you.

In those difficult times, trust that God will see you through. Believe that His plans for your future are for good. Know that even though something caught you off guard, it didn't catch God off guard. He is prepared and ready to lead you to the place of victory.

A Prayer for Today

Father, thank You for Your love and mercy in my life. Thank You that Your plan is to prosper me and to give me a hope and a future. I know that You see every unexpected and uncertain circumstance in my life. Thank You for watching over my life and protecting me. I declare You are directing my steps every day and orchestrating my life! I trust that You will go before me and prepare the way for victory in Jesus' Name. Amen.

Wake-Up Thought

Whatever you may have been experiencing, today is a brand-new day. We serve the Most High God, and His dream for your life is so much bigger and better than you can even imagine. He wants to do big things and new things in your life. Never settle for a small view of God. Start thinking as God thinks. Think big. Think increase. Think breakthrough. Think victory!

Now I Can See

Today's Scripture

> The man who had been blind said to them, "I do not know if He is a sinner or not. One thing I know. I was blind, but now I can see."
>
> JOHN 9:25 NLT

One time, Jesus healed a blind man, and the religious crowd got upset. They started arguing over why he was healed, how he was healed, and who was to blame for him being blind in the first place! They were hounding the man with questions. Finally, the man said, "Listen, guys. You all are confusing me. I can't answer all of your questions. All I can tell you is this: I was blind, but now I can see." He was saying, in effect, the proof of the pudding is in the eating! He was saying, "You can argue all day long, but I know the reason I can see is because of God's healing in my life."

There are people today who don't think you are supposed to be blessed. They don't think that God wants people to prosper and live in victory. But it's too late because we've already experienced His blessing. He's already opened up supernatural doors! We've seen His favor! Don't let the naysayers talk you out of your blessing. Don't let them convince you that God's Word isn't true. He's already done so much in your past, and He'll do more in your future. Keep standing, keep believing, and keep hoping.

Soon you'll see His blessing in every area of your life!

A Prayer for Today

Father in Heaven, I love You and praise Your holy Name. Thank You for Your abundant blessings in my life. Thank You for opening the eyes of my heart so that I can, first of all, see You and then see every good thing You have in store for me. I look to You with an attitude of faith and expectancy and believe that You are at work in me in Jesus' Name! Amen.

Wake-Up Thought

To "prosper" means having your health, having peace in your mind, being able to sleep at night, having good relationships, having the finances you need. Scripture never suggests we are supposed to drag around not having enough. Jesus came that we might live an abundant life. We represent Almighty God here on this earth. We should be such examples of His goodness—so blessed, so prosperous, so generous, so full of joy—that other people want what we have.

The Way to Enter

Today's Scripture

> *Enter into His gates with thanksgiving, and into His courts with praise. Be thankful to Him, and bless His name.*
>
> PSALM 100:4 NKJV

What an amazing privilege we have to enter boldly into His throne of grace. We serve a personal God who desires a relationship with us. We have access to Him 24 hours a day, 7 days a week, 365 days a year! But notice that today's verse tells us that we shouldn't just come to Him any old way. We shouldn't come empty-handed to the King of kings and the Lord of lords. What do we have to give that's worthy of Almighty God? Our praise. Our thanksgiving. Our worship. We should always enter His gates with an offering of adoration from our hearts.

Praise isn't just about singing songs in church. Praise is the expression of gratefulness to God for Who He is and all that He has done. Praise gets God's attention. Praise is a powerful tool in the life of the believer because God inhabits the praises of His people! When we enter His presence the right way, He enters our circumstances; and when God shows up, the enemy must flee! Today, enter into His gates with thanksgiving and open the door for Him to move on your behalf!

A Prayer for Today

Father, You alone are worthy of my praise. I come to You with a heart full of thanksgiving. I have so much to be grateful for because of Your goodness. You are good, and Your mercy endures forever! Thank You for doing exceedingly, abundantly above all I could ever ask or imagine. Have Your way in my life, for I desire to please You and live for You. I honor You today and submit every area of my life to You in Jesus' Name. Amen.

Wake-Up Thought

It is good to start off your day by thanking God for who He is and all that He has done for you. Begin by thanking God for the basics: "Father, thank You for my health. Thank You for my children. Thank You for my family. Thank You for my home. Father, thank You for all that You've done for me." Your praise is what gets God's attention and activates His favor.

This Is the Will of God for You

Today's Scripture

> *Give thanks in all circumstances; for this is God's will for you in Christ Jesus.*
>
> 1 THESSALONIANS 5:18 NIV

So many people today wonder what God's will is for their lives. Oftentimes, they look for big things, signs and supernatural events. But really, God's will for us unfolds each and every day as we obey Him and serve Him with a thankful heart.

When you wake up every morning with an attitude of praise and thanksgiving, you just took a step toward your destiny—you are walking in the will of God. When you go throughout your day thanking God that His hand of blessing is upon you, thanking Him for ordering your steps, thanking Him for a new day, you are taking another step in His will.

Today, remember to keep the right perspective. We should have goals and dreams and look forward to a bright future, but the way you live your life today is what's going to get you to where you need to be tomorrow. Keep praising, keep believing, and keep thanking Him, because that's what will keep you moving forward. Submit every area of your life to Him and walk forward into victory.

A Prayer for Today

Father, I come to You today with thanksgiving in my heart and a mouth full of praise! I worship You because You are worthy Almighty God! Thank You for redeeming and restoring my life. Help me to keep the right perspective and maintain an attitude of thanksgiving. Thank You for leading me in the way everlasting as I keep my heart and mind on You today in Jesus' Name. Amen.

Wake-Up Thought

No matter what comes against you, have a grateful attitude. You may be facing some formidable obstacles in your path. But if you look hard enough you can find some reason to be grateful. The Scripture says to give thanks "in all circumstances"; it doesn't say "for all circumstances." You don't necessarily thank God for your problems; you thank God in spite of your problems, looking for the good in every situation.

Focus on What You Have

Today's Scripture

> *Here is what I have seen: It is good and fitting for one to eat and drink, and to enjoy the good of all his labor in which he toils under the sun all the days of his life which God gives him; for it is his heritage.*

ECCLESIASTES 5:18 NKJV

The Scripture talks about how God has given us the power to enjoy what is allotted to us. That simply means another person doesn't have the power to enjoy your life. You may have more success, more money, more friends, and a better job, but if you put another person in your life, they are not going to enjoy it as you do. We are each uniquely designed to run our own race.

When we truly understand and embrace this, we won't be tempted to compare or wish we had what someone else has. You won't think, *If only I had their talent...* No, if God wanted you to have that talent, He would have given it to you. Instead, take what you have and develop it. Make the most of it. Don't think, *If only I had her looks...* No, God gave you your looks. That's not an accident. The life you have has been perfectly matched for you.

Now, you have to do your part and get excited about your life. Be excited about who you are—your looks, your talent, your ability, your personality. When you're passionate about who you are, it brings honor to God. That's when God will breathe in your direction and the seeds of greatness in you will take root and begin to flourish!

A Prayer for Today

Father God, I love You and appreciate You. I thank You for giving me the gifts, talents, and abilities to enjoy life and accomplish Your will. I will not criticize who I am, but celebrate who I am. Thank You for uniquely designing me to run my race. I declare that You have placed greatness in me and I will flourish! I put my trust and hope in You, knowing that You have equipped me for the destiny You have for me in Jesus' Name. Amen.

Wake-Up Thought

Really, it's an insult to God to wish you were someone else. You are saying, "God, why did you make me subpar? Why did you make me less than others?" God didn't make anyone inferior. He didn't create anyone to be second-class. You are a masterpiece. You are fully loaded and totally equipped for the race that's designed for you. It's easy to run your race because you're equipped for what you need.

Eternal Glory

Today's Scripture

> *For our light and momentary troubles are achieving for us an eternal glory that far outweighs them all.*

2 CORINTHIANS 4:17 NIV

Troubles and trials are only temporary! In fact, this verse tells us they are momentary. Compared with eternity, our troubles won't last long at all! When you stand strong in faith during the difficult times, you are building faith in your life and also achieving eternal glory.

If you are in the middle of tough times today, look to God. The Bible says that He is the Author and Finisher of our faith. He is the one who writes faith on your heart and then develops it to completion on the inside of you. Your part is to open your heart and choose those words of faith and victory.

Remember, your words set the course for your life. As you remind yourself that your troubles are only momentary and declare your trust and hope in God, you will see His hand moving in your life. It won't be long until you're past those momentary troubles and experiencing His eternal glory!

A Prayer for Today

Heavenly Father, thank You for Your eternal glory at work in me. I know my trials and troubles are only temporary. I cast my cares on You because You promised to sustain me. Help me stand strong on Your Word and develop my faith. I declare my faith is strong and victory is mine! Thank You for Your eternal blessing on every area of my life in Jesus' Name! Amen.

Wake-Up Thought

When it comes to troubles, you need to have one of those posted signs that says, "No Vacancy Here."  *In your mind, don't let tough times move in and take up residency. They are not a part of who you are. God is saying, "It's not permanent; it's temporary. It didn't come to stay; it came to pass." You need to be saying, "This may be where I am, but it is not who I am. I am blessed. I am healthy. I am strong. I am victorious."*

Receive Grace

Today's Scripture

> *It is through Him that we have received grace (God's unmerited favor) and [our] apostleship to promote obedience to the faith and make disciples for His name's sake among all the nations.*
>
> ROMANS 1:5 AMPC

Do you want to see more of God's favor in your life? Receive His grace. Grace is God's favor, but it's also His supernatural empowerment. When you have God's grace and favor, it enables you to accomplish more and be more effective both in your own life and in building the kingdom of God.

This verse says that God's grace enables us to promote obedience to the faith and make disciples among all nations. Maybe you can't go to all nations today, but you can make a difference in the lives of the people around you. You can "promote faith" by being an example to others. God wants to empower you with His grace so that you can show love and encourage the people in your life—your coworkers, your family, your friends.

Receive His grace today by simply opening your heart and thanking Him for it. Thank Him for His grace that empowers you. Thank Him for His gift of faith in your life. Let Him empower you to walk forward in the favor and blessing He has prepared!

A Prayer for Today

Father, I love You and praise Your holy Name. Thank You for empowering me with your unlimited grace to do all You have called me to do. Thank You for Your unmerited favor and supernatural strength. I receive Your grace and power right now and invite Your love to flow through me today in Jesus' Name. Amen.

Wake-Up Thought

When you are empowered to walk forward in grace, your life gives praise to God. That's one of the best witnesses you can have. Some people will never go to church or listen to a sermon. They're not reading the Bible. Instead, they're reading your life. They're watching how you live. Make sure you give them the best example you possibly can. You're representing Almighty God.

Prepared Blessings

Today's Scripture

You prepare a table before me.

PSALM 23:5 NIV

When God laid out the plan for your life, He lined up the right people, the right breaks, and the right opportunities. He has blessings that have your name on them. If you will stay in faith and keep honoring God, one day you will come into what already belongs to you. It's a prepared blessing!

Think about Adam and Eve in the garden. God took the first five days and created the heavens, the earth, the sky, the land, and the water. He planted a garden. He put in it beautiful flowers and luscious fruit. He designed rivers to flow through it. He put precious treasures in the ground: onyx, gold, and silver. Then Scripture says, "He took Adam, whom He had just breathed life into, and put him in the garden." Notice Adam came into a prepared blessing, something that God had already finished for him.

In the same way, God has some prepared blessings in store for you. He is working behind the scenes, arranging things in your favor, getting it all perfectly in place. You couldn't make it happen on your own. It's just the goodness of God bringing you into a prepared blessing!

A Prayer for Today

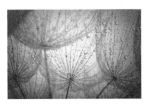

Father, I praise and thank You today for all Your blessings. Thank You for preparing a place of blessing for me and for arranging things in my favor. I choose to trust You and Your timing, knowing that You are working behind the scenes on my behalf. I declare that I am coming into my prepared blessings and You are lining up the right people, breaks, and opportunities in Jesus' Name! Amen.

Wake-Up Thought

It's time to step up to God's dining table and dig in to the fabulous blessings He has prepared for you, complete with every good thing imaginable. God has everything you need—joy, forgiveness, restoration, peace, healing—anything you need to live at your full potential. If you'll pull up your chair and take your place at God's banquet table, He has it all prepared and waiting for you. Best of all, the price has already been paid.

What Are You Considering?

Today's Scripture

> And not being weak in faith, he
> did not consider his own body...
> He did not waver at the promise
> of God through unbelief, but was
> strengthened in faith, giving glory
> to God, and being fully convinced
> that what He had promised He
> was also able to perform.
>
> ROMANS 4:19–21 NKJV

Abraham had many obstacles coming against the promise of God in his life. God told him that he would be "the father of many nations." Abraham was over ninety years old before he ever saw that promise begin to come to pass. This Scripture tells us that he didn't consider his body. He didn't think and meditate on all the reasons he couldn't be the father of many nations. No, he considered and thought about the strength and ability of God! He thought about God's faithfulness and gave praise and glory to Him. Abraham exercised faith that enabled God to move on His behalf.

What are you believing God for? Does it seem impossible? Is it taking a long time? Consider your God. Consider His Word. Consider His faithfulness. Just like Abraham, you'll grow strong as you give glory to God. Your faith will open the door for God to move in every area of your life!

A Prayer for Today

Father, thank You for Your faithfulness and strength at work in my life today. I choose to consider Your ability over my circumstances. I may be limited, but You are never limited. I choose to trust You because I know what is impossible with me is possible with You. I give You all the praise, honor, and glory, now and always in Jesus' Name. Amen.

Wake-Up Thought

Like Abraham, there will be times when it seems as if your dreams are not coming to pass. It's taking so long. When you run the numbers, it may not seem logical. Business is slow. You could easily give up. That's one report, but God has another report. He's saying, "What I have spoken over your life I will bring to pass. What I have promised I will do." Believe that God is in control.

Change Your Mind

Today's Scripture

And saying, Repent (think differently; change your mind, regretting your sins and changing your conduct), for the kingdom of heaven is at hand.

MATTHEW 3:2 AMPC

Do you have behaviors in your life that you want to change? Maybe it's a habit, a bad attitude, or even negative thoughts. No matter what you may want to change in your life, you have to start by changing your mind. You have to change your thinking so that your thoughts are in line with God's thoughts. When you make the decision to follow God in every area of your life, you open the door for His supernatural power to work.

Remember, your life will go in the direction of your thoughts. You can't just allow any old thought or image to play in your mind. You have to choose right thoughts. The easiest way to change your thoughts is by speaking God's Word. When you say "orange," you probably won't start thinking about an apple. In the same way, when you confess the Word of God, which says you are more than a conqueror, it will drive those negative, defeating thoughts away! Change your mind today by changing your words!

A Prayer for Today

Heavenly Father, I love You and praise You. Today I choose to take captive every thought that is contrary to Your Word and Your will. I repent for anything in my life that is displeasing to You. Help me to guard my mind and my heart and to dwell on Your thoughts. Help me to be strong to resist temptation and compromise. I thank You that I have the power of the Holy Spirit in me to help me live a victorious life in Jesus' Name. Amen.

Wake-Up Thought

There is a miracle in your mouth. If you want to change your mind, start by changing your words. When you're facing obstacles in your path,  *you must boldly say, "Greater is He who is in me than he who is in the world"; "No weapon formed against me is going to prosper"; and "God always causes me to triumph." The moment you speak something out, you give birth to it. Your words have that power.*

What He Says about You

Today's Scripture

> *That is why, for Christ's sake, I delight in weaknesses, in insults, in hardships, in persecutions, in difficulties. For when I am weak, then I am strong.*
>
> 2 CORINTHIANS 12:10 NIV

A man in Scripture by the name of Gideon was called by God to lead the people of Israel against an opposing army. But Gideon didn't think he was capable.

One day, the angel of the Lord appeared to him and said, "Hello, Gideon, you mighty man of fearless courage." It's easy to imagine Gideon was looking around thinking, *Who is He talking to? I am not a mighty man of fearless courage.* Gideon was afraid, intimidated, and insecure; just the opposite. But notice, God didn't call him what he was. God called him what he could become.

Today, know that God sees your potential. He knows what you're capable of. You may feel weak, but God calls you strong. You may be intimidated, but God calls you confident. You may feel less than, but God calls you well able. Get in agreement with God and start believing what He says about you!

A Prayer for Today

*Father, today I give You all the praise and
glory. I receive Your words of life, strength,
and encouragement. I choose to see myself
the way You see me. I declare I am full of
potential and greatness! I choose to walk
in the way that You have prepared for me.
Thank You for loving me and seeing the best
in me in Jesus' Name. Amen.*

Wake-Up Thought

*You may feel that you're average. You may
think you're ordinary, but God sees you as a
champion. He believes in you and regards
you as a strong, courageous, successful,
overcoming person. You may not see yourself
that way, but that doesn't change God's
image of you. God still sees you exactly as
His Word describes you. Dare to start seeing
yourself as God sees you—as a victor!*

Don't Be Defined by the Limits of Others

Today's Scripture

> *Your word, LORD, is eternal;*
> *it stands firm in the heavens.*
>
> PSALM 119:89 NIV

Most people's thoughts were programmed by the people who raised them or by what somebody spoke over them. Maybe they were good people, doing the best they could, but their words have limited you. As long as you believe what they said about you, their words are defining you. The key to breaking those limitations is to start meditating on what God says about you. A transformation will take place when you renew your mind. Reprogram your thinking with what God says about you. God says, "The path of the righteous gets brighter and brighter." All through the day say, "I'm rising higher. I haven't seen my best days. Something good is going to happen to me."

As you meditate on His Word day in and day out, you're breaking out of the past limitations set by others. People may have spoken negative things over you, but the good news is that people don't determine your destiny. You are not who people say you are. You are who God says you are. Don't be defined by the limits of others. Believe God's Word and see His victory all the days of your life!

A Prayer for Today

Father in Heaven, I praise Your holy Name. Today I choose to believe Your Word over the words of others. You are the One who defines my life and destiny. Search my heart; search my mind. Show me any areas where I need to be renewed to Your Word. I declare that I am rising higher and something good is going to happen to me in Jesus' Name. Amen.

Wake-Up Thought

Have you allowed what somebody—a coach, a teacher, a parent, an ex-spouse—said about you to hold you back? They've planted negative seeds of what you cannot do. "You're not smart enough. You're not talented enough. You're not disciplined enough. You're not attractive enough. You'll always make Cs. You'll always struggle with your weight." Get rid of those lies! Let the seeds of greatness God has placed on the inside spring forth.

God Looks Beyond the Surface

Today's Scripture

> *"The LORD does not look at the
> things people look at. People
> look at the outward appearance,
> but the LORD looks at the heart."*
>
> 1 SAMUEL 16:7 NIV

Your Creator can see things in you that other people cannot see. Sometimes people will try to push you down or make you feel insignificant. Sometimes your own thoughts will try to convince you that you don't measure up. But God looks beyond the surface, beyond the mistakes you've made, beyond what somebody said about you, and He sees your incredible value. You may think, *I've messed up. I have blown it. I have failed. I'm all washed up.* No, God still sees more in you. God doesn't just see what you are; He sees what you can become. You may have made some mistakes, but God still sees victory on the inside of you. People may have tried to push you down, but God sees you rising higher.

Now, you have to do your part and get rid of those condemning thoughts. Get rid of what somebody has spoken over you and start renewing your mind. Down deep, start believing that you are redeemed, restored, talented, and valuable. Even if you have made mistakes, believe that there is more in store.

God's not finished with you. He looks beyond the surface and sees your potential. Stay in step with Him and watch His plan for your life unfold.

A Prayer for Today

Father, I praise You and thank You for looking beyond the surface and seeing the real me. Thank You for placing potential and greatness on the inside of me. I break off all negative and condemning thoughts today! Help me to know You more and see You more clearly so I can follow Your ways all the days of my life in Jesus' Name. Amen.

Wake-Up Thought

When God made you, He stepped back and said, "I like that. That was good. Another masterpiece!" He stamped His approval on you. Other people may disapprove of you. Don't go around feeling less than, feeling inferior. Our attitude should be: I am approved by Almighty God. I am accepted. I am a masterpiece.

Overcome the World

Today's Scripture

> *I have told you these things, so that in Me you may have [perfect] peace and confidence. In the world you have tribulation and trials and distress and frustration; but be of good cheer [take courage; be confident, certain, undaunted]! For I have overcome the world. [I have deprived it of power to harm you and have conquered it for you.]*
>
> JOHN 16:33 AMPC

When trials and tribulations come, as children of the Most High God, we can take courage. We can be confident, and we can have perfect peace. Why? Because perfect peace doesn't come from the world. Courage doesn't come from the world, and neither does confidence. These things come from a relationship with Almighty God. We can have hope in challenging times because

God has promised us victory. As long as we stay in faith, as long as we put our trust and hope in God, we will stay in victory.

No matter what you are facing today, remember, faith pleases God and opens the door for His supernatural favor, strength, and wisdom. Don't settle for defeat, because you are preprogrammed for victory. Choose to thank Him for what He is doing in your life and for the victory that is on the way. Be strong, be bold, and take courage today because God has overcome the world!

A Prayer for Today

Father in Heaven, thank You for loving me and setting me free. Thank You for Your promise of peace and victory in every area of my life. I declare I am bold and strong and courageous to do all God has called me to do! I choose to keep my mind focused on You, knowing that You always cause me to triumph in Jesus' Name. Amen.

Wake-Up Thought

When you face adversity, have the attitude of a victor. You may be weary and tired, worn down, and ready to give up. You must act  *on your will, not simply your emotions. Sometimes that means you have to take steps of faith even when you are hurting, grieving, or still reeling from some attack of the enemy. Keep standing up on the inside and God will step in and do what you can't do.*

Living Full of God

Today's Scripture

> *"You shall go out with joy,
> and be led out with peace."*
>
> ISAIAH 55:12 NKJV

The word *enthusiasm* comes from the Greek word *entheos. Theos* is God. When you're enthusiastic, it simply means you are full of God. When you get up in the morning excited about your future, recognizing that this day is a gift, and go out with a spring in your step, pursuing your goals, passionate about life, then God will breathe in your direction. Studies tell us that people who are enthusiastic get better breaks. They're promoted more often. That's not a coincidence. When you're full of passion, you have the favor of God.

Remember, God didn't breathe His life into us to drag through the day. He didn't create us in His image, crown us with His favor, and equip us with His power to just go through the motions of life. You may have had some setbacks, the wind may have been taken out of your sail, but this is a new day! God wants to breathe new life back into you. If you'll get your fire and passion back, the wind will start blowing once again. When you're in agreement with God, He can cause the winds of favor to shift in your direction!

A Prayer for Today

Father, thank You for another day, another opportunity to praise You and pursue the dreams You have given me. Help me to stay filled with Your joy, enthusiasm, and passion each and every day. I declare I am equipped and empowered to do Your will! Thank You for giving me favor and causing me to be promoted as I serve You with my whole heart in Jesus' Name. Amen.

Wake-Up Thought

My question for you is this: are you really alive? Are you passionate about your life or are you stuck in a rut, letting the pressures of life weigh you down, or taking for granted what you have? You have seeds of greatness on the inside. There's something more for you to accomplish. Stir up the enthusiasm and passion, and your faith will allow God to do amazing things.

Further Faster

Today's Scripture

> *But do not forget this one thing, dear friends: with the Lord a day is like a thousand years, and a thousand years are like a day.*
>
> 2 PETER 3:8 NIV

We believe God wants to do exceedingly, abundantly above and beyond what you could even ask or think. He can take you further faster than you could ever dream. God can speed things up on your behalf. Because you honor and trust Him, things that should have taken you a lifetime to accomplish will only take you a fraction of the time. This is the kind of God we serve!

We see this all through Scripture. In just one day, David went from a shepherd boy to the one who led the Israelite army to victory. Ruth was a poor widow collecting scraps in the field, and

God sent her to Boaz. She went from begging in the field to owning the field. God breathed in her direction. God took her further faster.

Remember, the thoughts you think and the words you say are prophesying your future. If you want to see a shift occur in your life, you have to get in agreement with God and say, "Yes, God, this is for me. I thank You that I am coming into my destiny sooner than I imagined!"

A Prayer for Today

Father, this is the day that You have made and I will rejoice and be glad in it. I choose to trust that You are  *working behind the scenes on my behalf. I believe that You can take me further faster than I could ever imagine because I honor You. I prophesy and declare that my future is bright and I am fulfilling my destiny! I surrender every area of my life to You. Use me for Your glory in Jesus' Name. Amen.*

Wake-Up Thought

In your career, maybe it should take you twenty years to work your way up to that desired position. No, things have shifted. God will bring the right people and opportunities across your path. It will take you further faster. Get those two words planted down in your spirit. It may look in the natural as though it will take you years to get out of debt, years to get well, years to overcome that problem. No, you need to get ready. You've come into this shift.

He Makes Up the Difference

Today's Scripture

> *So for the sake of Christ, I am well pleased and take pleasure in infirmities, insults, hardships, persecutions, perplexities and distresses; for when I am weak [in human strength], then am I [truly] strong (able, powerful in divine strength).*

2 CORINTHIANS 12:10 AMPC

No matter what weakness you think you may have, no matter what inadequacies or setbacks you've encountered, God wants to give you His divine strength. He wants to make up the difference and put you further ahead than you ever thought possible.

One time in the Old Testament, God simply multiplied the sound of four men's footsteps and caused them to sound like a mighty army. When their enemies heard them, they took off running. There were thousands of enemy troops running for their lives, scared to death, thinking they were being attacked by a massive army when, in fact, it was just four people! What happened? God made up the difference.

God can make you seem bigger than you really are. He can make you look more powerful. He knows how to multiply your influence, your strength, your talent, and your income. You don't have to figure it all out; all you have to do is put your trust in Him. If you will trust Him and wake up every day expecting His far and beyond favor, you're going to see Him make up the difference in every area of your life!

A Prayer for Today

Heavenly Father, I love You and appreciate all You have done for me. Today I commit every area of my life to You. I know that you are not limited because of my inadequacies or setbacks! I am confident that You will make up the difference and supply everything I need to fulfill Your purposes in my life. I declare that I am strong in You and in the power of Your might in Jesus' Name. Amen.

Wake-Up Thought

God loves to use ordinary people, faults and all, to do extraordinary things. Are you allowing your weaknesses and insecurities to keep you from being your best? Are you letting feelings of inadequacy keep you from believing God for bigger things? God wants to use you in spite of your weaknesses. Don't focus on your weaknesses; focus on your God.

Hope

And so, Lord, where do I put my hope? My only hope is in you.

PSALM 39:7 NLT

Blessed Beyond Your Wildest Dreams

Today's Scripture

> *Is any thing too hard for the* LORD?
>
> GENESIS 18:14 KJV

In Genesis, God promised Sarah that she was going to have a child. At first she didn't believe it. She thought she was too old. She thought her time had passed. But do you know what God said to her? He simply asked, "Sarah, is there anything too hard for the Lord?" We believe God is saying the same thing to us today. "Is there anything too hard for Me?"

Do you think your dreams are too big for God to bring to pass? Do you think that a relationship is too far gone for God to restore it? Do you think you have to live with sickness the rest of your life? Get a new vision today because there is nothing too hard for God! God is saying today, "I am all-powerful. I can turn any situation around." It doesn't matter what things look like in the natural, we serve a supernatural God. The Amplified Bible, Classic Edition puts it this way, "Is anything too hard or too wonderful for the Lord?"

The next time you think, *That's just too good to be true,* remember, God wants to bless you beyond your wildest dreams. Take the limits off and dare to believe that He has wonderful things in store for you!

A Prayer for Today

Father in Heaven, thank You for Your love and kindness in my life. Today I choose to trust You with my whole heart. I know there is nothing too hard for You. I take off all the limits and believe that You have wonderful things in store for me! Thank You for blessing me beyond my wildest dreams! Help me to stand strong in faith and stay close to You all the days of my life in Jesus' Name. Amen.

Wake-Up Thought

God is saying, "If you'll take the limits off Me, I'll amaze you with My goodness. I'll not only meet your needs, I'll take it one step further. I'll give you the desires of your heart." These are the secret petitions of your heart, the hidden dreams that you haven't told anybody about. It's just between you and God. Know this today: God wants to bring your secret petitions to pass. Will you put your faith out there?

Who Do You Agree With?

Today's Scripture

> *"Again, truly I tell you that if two of you on earth agree about anything they ask for, it will be done for them by my Father in heaven."*
>
> MATTHEW 18:19 NIV

The Scripture talks about how when any two of us agree, it shall be done. That's a promise that when we stand in faith with another believer, God will do what He said. Well, we believe that principle is true even in the negative. When the enemy puts a thought in your mind, if you agree, your agreement is what gives it the power to come to pass. But if you don't agree, you turn it around.

The thought says, *Your children are going to get into trouble.* But you respond, *No, I don't agree. My children will be mighty in the land.*

My children will fulfill their destiny. You've just stopped that fear from coming to pass. The thought says, *You'd better not go out today. You're going to have an accident.* You answer, *No, I don't agree. God has a hedge of protection around me and gives His angels charge over me.*

Here's the key: don't come into agreement with the fear. If you don't agree, the only way it can come to pass is if God gives it permission. And if God does, you can rest assured it's not going to work against you. It's going to work for you. Today, pay attention to what you're coming into agreement with and don't agree with fear. Agree with God's Word and embrace the good things He has in store for you.

A Prayer for Today

Father, I give You all the glory and honor. Today I come into agreement with You. Thank You for the good things that You have in store for me. I choose to align my words, my thoughts, and my actions with Your Word, which is a lamp to my feet and a light to my path. I will hide Your Word in my heart that I might not sin against You in Jesus' Name. Amen.

Wake-Up Thought

When you get in agreement with God, the victory will come because God smiles down on you. Don't keep dwelling on everything you lack, the mistakes you've made, or the greater talents of the competition. You're just looking at what's visible, but there is something about you that cannot be measured, something that goes beyond your talent, your education, or your ability. It's the favor of Almighty God.

Catch the Wave

Today's Scripture

> *Deep calls to deep in the roar of your waterfalls; all your waves and breakers have swept over me.*
>
> PSALM 42:7 NIV

God wants to release a flood of His power in your life. Not a trickle, not a stream, not a river, but a flood—a flood of increase, a flood of healing, a flood of ideas. Don't get stuck in a rut believing for small things. Don't settle for where you are because you think you've reached your limits. No, you need to get ready. See something in your future. Through eyes of faith you can see a tidal wave coming your way. It's not a wave of defeat, a wave of bad breaks, a wave of more of the same. No, things have shifted. It's a wave of increase, a wave of favor, a wave of healing! It's God releasing His goodness like a flood. It's going to help you to overcome that obstacle. It's going to cause you to accomplish your dreams.

Today, why don't you dare to believe? Don't just think *trickle*. Switch over into faith and start thinking *flood*. If you'll believe for His overflow, God can bring you into overflow. If you'll dare to believe *tidal wave*, God will release a tidal wave of His goodness in your life!

A Prayer for Today

Father God, thank You for another day to praise You. Today I lift my heart to You to receive the tidal wave of goodness You have prepared for me. I thank You for releasing a flood of Your power in my life and bringing me into overflow. Help me keep my eyes on Your supernatural provision and overcome every obstacle. Thank You for victory in Jesus' Name. Amen.

Wake-Up Thought

You may be accepting things in your life that are far less than God's best. You've done that so long you don't see how it could change. But this is a new day. New seeds have taken root in your heart. And the good news is the God of the breakthrough is about to visit you. Release your faith in a greater way. Like a flood, His favor can overtake you. Don't ever rule out the God of the breakthrough.

Unlimited Supply

Today's Scripture

And [so that you can know and understand] what is the immeasurable and unlimited and surpassing greatness of His power in and for us who believe, as demonstrated in the working of His mighty strength.

Ephesians 1:19 AMPC

I f someone had a thousand gallons of water to give you but you only had a one-gallon container, you wouldn't be able to receive what they had for you. The problem would not be with the supply; it would be with your ability to receive. If you would get rid of the small container and get something larger, you could receive so much more.

It's the same way with God. You may think, *The economy is too down. I could never afford that house I really want. My business will never expand. I don't have the funding. I don't have the right people behind me.* No, you have to get rid of that one-gallon bucket. Get rid of that small container. The God we serve is a big God! He has an ocean, an unlimited supply. Jesus said, "According to your faith it will be done unto you." It's not according to God. God has all the power, all the resources in the world. It's according to what we believe. Today, increase your capacity to receive. Enlarge your thinking by meditating on the Word of God. Praise Him and magnify Him, because with God, all things are possible, and He has an unlimited supply!

A Prayer for Today

Father in Heaven, I love You and praise You. Thank You for Your unlimited supply of everything I need in this life. I open my heart to You and increase my capacity to receive. I choose to take the limits off because I know all things are possible to You. I praise You and thank You for Your goodness in my life in Jesus' Name. Amen.

Wake-Up Thought

The Scripture says, "Open your mouth wide and I will fill it." My question is this: "Do you have your mouth opened wide? What are you expecting? Do you believe in increase? Do you go out each day knowing that favor is in your future or are you stuck in a rut?" If you'll take the limits off of God—if you'll get up every morning expecting far-and-beyond favor—He won't disappoint you.

Don't Miss Your Moment

Today's Scripture

> *Jesus turned and saw her. "Take heart, daughter," he said, "your faith has healed you." And the woman was healed at that moment.*
>
> MATTHEW 9:22 NIV

In Scripture, there was a lady who had been sick with a bleeding disorder for twelve years. She went to the best doctors, received the finest treatment, but her health continued to decline. One day, she got word that Jesus was coming through her town. When she heard that, something came alive on the inside. She had so much coming against her, but she didn't focus on that; she knew it was her time for healing. Instead of giving up, she fought her way through the crowds and touched the edge of Jesus' robe. When she did, immediately she was made whole.

How many other people were there like her in that same type of situation? They were sick. They were discouraged. They had trouble. But they just watched Jesus pass by. They let excuses keep them from their miracle.

Don't let that be you. Don't let your circumstances keep you from reaching out to Jesus. It doesn't matter what's happened in your past, just keep moving forward. God has destiny moments in store for you. Keep pressing in, keep believing, keep praying, and, like this woman, reach out to Him. Know that He is faithful, and He will meet your faith with His power.

A Prayer for Today

Father, You are worthy to receive all glory and praise. Today I press into You with my faith. I believe that You have my miracle in the palm of Your hand. You have destiny moments for me. I choose to take my eyes off of my circumstances and set my gaze on You, Jesus, because You are the Author and Finisher of my faith in Jesus' Name. Amen.

Wake-Up Thought

Remember, the enemy always fights the hardest when he knows God has something great in store for you. The darkest battle, the darkest storm, will always give way to the brightest sunrise. The Scripture says to not grow weary or become discouraged for at the proper time we will reap, if we do not give in. It may be hard right now, but remind yourself that you have the power of God inside you to do what you need to do.

Put Your Love into Action

Today's Scripture

> *But if anyone has this world's goods (resources for sustaining life) and sees his brother and fellow believer in need, yet closes his heart of compassion against him, how can the love of God live and remain in him? Little children, let us not love [merely] in theory or in speech but in deed and in truth (in practice and in sincerity).*
>
> 1 JOHN 3:17–18 AMPC

It has been said that you can give without loving, but you can't love without giving. Notice this verse tells us that love isn't just about our words or thoughts; it's about our actions. Love is about reaching out and meeting the needs of others. Sometimes meeting someone's needs is as simple as a smile or sharing a word of encouragement. There are many ways to show the love of God. Can you pay for someone's gas or groceries? Do you see a need in someone's life that you can meet? The Lord wants to bless you today so that you can be a blessing to others. He wants to work through you to show His love and compassion.

Today and every day, look for ways to put your love into action. The Bible says that it's His kindness that leads people to repentance. He wants to show His kindness in the earth through you. Step out and sow good seeds of love by meeting the needs of others. God promises that those seeds will produce an abundant harvest in your life in return!

A Prayer for Today

Heavenly Father, thank You for Your hand of blessing in my life. I ask You to work through me today. I submit myself and my resources to You. Give me opportunities to put my love and kindness to action. Show me ways to be a blessing to others so that they can experience Your love in Jesus' Name. Amen.

Wake-Up Thought

If you study the life of Jesus, you will discover that He always took time for people. He was never so busy or unwilling to stop and help a person in need. His agenda was God's agenda. Certainly, when God created us, He put His supernatural love in all of our hearts. You have the opportunity to make a difference in other people's lives. You must learn to follow that love. Don't ignore it. Act on it. Somebody needs what you have.

Always Rise to the Top

Today's Scripture

> And the LORD was with Joseph,
> and he was a prosperous man.
>
> GENESIS 39:2 KJV

In Scripture, many heroes of the faith started out at the very bottom. Think of Joseph. He was thrown in a pit and sold into slavery by his own brothers. But even as a slave, he developed his skills. He was so valuable that he was put in charge of his master's whole household.

When he was falsely accused and put into prison, he was so valuable there that they put him in charge of the whole prison. What is that? Cream rising to the top. When Pharaoh needed someone to run the country and administer the nationwide feeding program during the famine, he didn't choose a cabinet member; he didn't choose his department head. He chose Joseph, a prisoner, a slave. Why? Joseph developed his skills right where he was. His gifts made room for him, and he was always rising to the top.

There's never an excuse to not keep rising. It doesn't matter if you don't like your current job; it doesn't matter if other people don't treat you right. God is saying, "It's time to get out of the pit. It's time to shake off the past. It's time to rise to the top!"

A Prayer for Today

Father, thank You for the gifts and talents that are within me. I let go of all my excuses today and I choose to  *have an excellent spirit. I choose to be a blessing everywhere I go, no matter what my situation. I take my eyes off of my circumstances and lift my eyes to You, knowing that You are the One who lifts me up. Thank You for causing me to rise to the top in Jesus' Name. Amen.*

Wake-Up Thought

Joseph was invaluable wherever he went because he learned to be a problem solver. He was solution oriented. Don't go to your boss with a list of problems unless you are prepared to present a list of solutions as well. Ask God for wisdom and offer solutions. You should be so productive, so filled with wisdom that no matter where you are, like Joseph, you will rise to the top.

Giant Slayer

Today's Scripture

> A man's gift makes room for him
> and brings him before great men.
>
> PROVERBS 18:16 NASB

When people hear the story of David and Goliath, sometimes they think, *That was all God.* And yes, in a sense, it was all God; but God didn't sling the stone. David had a role to play, too. God gave David the skill that he had to develop in order to be prepared for that defining moment.

Like David, God has put skills inside of you so that you can slay the giants in your life. You have the skills that can open new doors, skills that can lead to an abundant life, but the key is that the skills have to be developed. Every day that you spend growing, learning, and improving, you're getting prepared for that new level.

Today, while you're waiting for that new opportunity, start sharpening your skills. Study your boss. Study your manager. Learn that position. Be able to step into their shoes. When God sees that you are prepared, He can open new doors. The Scripture says, "Your gifts will make room for you." Keep developing your skills because there is a giant slayer in you!

A Prayer for Today

Father, I love You and worship You with all my heart. Thank You for depositing in me everything that I need for victory in my life. I choose to be faithful. I choose to sharpen my skills. Show me how I can improve and grow and be a blessing to others. Help me be prepared for every opportunity You have for my future in Jesus' Name. Amen.

Wake-Up Thought

When God sought somebody to defeat a giant, somebody to lead His chosen people, He looked to see who had taken the time to cultivate the gifts He had put in them. This is a call to action. There are new levels in your future. Things have shifted in your favor. God is looking for you to be prepared and to take steps to improve. He is looking for you to be serious about fulfilling your destiny.

Develop Your Talent

Today's Scripture

> *That you may walk (live and conduct yourselves) in a manner worthy of the Lord, fully pleasing to Him and desiring to please Him in all things, bearing fruit in every good work and steadily growing and increasing in and by the knowledge of God [with fuller, deeper, and clearer insight, acquaintance, and recognition].*

COLOSSIANS 1:10 AMPC

Too many people suffer from "destination disease." In other words, they've reached a certain level or obtained a goal, and now they're coasting in life off of what they've already learned. Studies tell us that 50 percent of people, after they graduate from high school, will never read an entire book the rest of their life. One reason is that people see learning as a period of life instead of a way of life. They think, *I'm out of school. I'm done with my training. I have my job.* But God never created us to reach one level and stop. Whether you're ninety years old or nine years old, you should be constantly learning, improving your skills, and getting better at what you do.

The key is that you have to take responsibility for your growth. Growth is not automatic. What steps are you taking to get better? Are you reading books? Listening to teaching CDs? Are you taking any courses on the Internet? Going to any seminars? Do you have any mentors? Don't just coast through life relying on what you've already learned. You have treasure on the inside. Develop your talent and become all that God created you to be.

A Prayer for Today

Father, thank You for Your love and kindness in my life. Help me to develop the talents You have given me. Show me how to continue growing, stretching, and increasing. Help me to maximize what You've placed in my hand and become all You have created me to be. Thank You for Your faithfulness in my life in Jesus' Name. Amen.

Wake-Up Thought

Winners never stop learning. Every one of us should have a personal growth plan. Not something vague: "I'll read a book every once in a while. I'll take the company training this year." No, you need a specific plan that lays out how you're going to grow. It should include the steps you will take to get better. When you take responsibility for your growth, God will honor your efforts.

The Completion Date Is Set

Today's Scripture

> *Being confident of this, that he who began a good work in you will carry it on to completion until the day of Christ Jesus.*
>
> PHILIPPIANS 1:6 NIV

God will always finish what He started. The moment God placed a dream in your heart, the moment that promise took root, God not only started something in your life but He also set a completion date. Scripture tells us that God is called the Author and the Finisher of our faith. God wouldn't have given you the dream, and the promise wouldn't have come alive, if God didn't already have a plan to bring it to pass.

It doesn't matter how long it's been or how impossible it looks. Your mind may tell you that it's too late. You've missed too many opportunities. It's never going to happen. No, God is saying, "It's not over. I have the final say. I've already set the completion date." So if you will stay in faith and not talk yourself out of it, it will just be a matter of time before it comes to pass!

A Prayer for Today

Father in Heaven, I love You and appreciate You. Thank You for completing what You've started in my life. I refuse to give up! I choose to trust You and wait on You. I declare that my dreams will come to pass in due season! I put my faith in You, knowing that through faith and patience every promise will come to pass in Jesus' Name. Amen.

Wake-Up Thought

The Message translation says "that the God who started this great work in you would keep at it and bring it to a flourishing finish on the very day Christ Jesus appears." That is not a defeated finish, where you barely make it and are beat up and broke. You are coming to a flourishing finish, a finish more rewarding than you ever imagined. When you have finishing grace, all the forces of darkness cannot stop you.

Walk Through

Today's Scripture

> *Even though I walk through the darkest valley, I will fear no evil, for you are with me; your rod and your staff, they comfort me.*
>
> PSALM 23:4 NIV

Sometimes in life, you have to play in pain. In other words, you have to keep going even when you don't feel like it. You have to keep pressing forward even when it's not easy. Every voice will tell you, "You're done. There's nothing good in your future." No, don't believe those lies. God sees your effort. It's one thing to do the right thing and make good decisions when everything is going your way. That's great. God honors that. When times are tough and nothing is going your way, when you're hurting, when you should be on the sidelines nursing your wound, instead, you're still in the game. You're still getting to work on time, you're still being good to someone, you're still expecting God to turn it around—that gets God's attention in a new way.

We believe God has a greater reward for people who are faithful in the tough times. If that's you today, know that God has His hand on you. He's walking with you through the valley. He's preparing streams in the desert. He's leading and guiding you in paths of righteousness for His Name's sake. Keep praising. Keep believing. Keep moving forward, knowing that God is with you, and His comfort will guide you to the place of blessing.

A Prayer for Today

Father, thank You for being my Good Shepherd and for caring for me. Thank You for walking with me in the valley, in the tough places. I will not fear because You are with me, comforting me. Goodness and mercy are following me all the days of my life. Thank You for restoring my soul and leading me to a place of victory and blessing in Jesus' Name. Amen.

Wake-Up Thought

If you are to become all God created you to be, you can't let an injury, hurt, or disappointment cause you to sit on the sidelines. Shake off the discouragement and get back in the game. Bandage up the wounds and hurts. Forgive the person who did you wrong. Let go of what didn't work out and get back in the game. No matter what life deals your way, your attitude should be: I'm hurting, but I'm still here.

Make Room for Something Greater

Today's Scripture

> *So the last shall be first, and the first last: for many are called, but few chosen.*
>
> MATTHEW 20:16 KJV

Before we are promoted in life, before we can be moved ahead, we have to be prepared. Sometimes it's a spiritual preparation. Sometimes it's a physical preparation, but we all go through seasons of preparation.

Too often, people miss their appointed time simply because they are not ready. They haven't prepared. They look around at others and think, *Well, they're more qualified than I am.* No, if you'll get ready, if you'll outgrow where you are, God will make room for something greater.

Don't worry about who's in line in front of you. You just keep growing, learning, and getting prepared, and the right doors will open. The fact is that God may not want you to have your supervisor's position. That may be too low for you. God may be about to thrust you right past them into a whole new level. You just be faithful to develop what God has placed in you, and He will take you further than you can ever imagine!

A Prayer for Today

Father, I praise Your holy Name. Today I open my heart and mind to the great things You have in store for my future. I choose to be faithful. I choose to prepare. I won't look to the left or to the right, but I will keep my eyes on You, Jesus. Thank You for opening the right doors for me and taking me further than I can imagine in Jesus' Name. Amen!

Wake-Up Thought

You might feel that your supervisors aren't going anywhere right now, but study your manager's work habits. Study your best supervisor. Learn how to do their job. Be ready to step into those shoes. If you outgrow them, outperform them, out produce them, and learn more than they know, your gifts will make room for you. Somewhere, somehow, and some way God will open a door and get you where He wants you to be.

Get Noticed

Today's Scripture

> *Do you see a man skillful in his work? He will stand before kings; he will not stand before obscure men.*
>
> PROVERBS 22:29 ESV

There was an article out recently that talked about how to reduce the risk of being laid off. There are three main things that employers look for when deciding who to keep. They want to keep people who are positive, people who are versatile, and people who are always improving.

Are you focused on developing your gifts in such a way that your company cannot make it without you? Do they notice that things don't run nearly as smoothly when you're not there? If you take a week off and nobody misses you, all the work gets done and sales are just as good, unless you're the owner, it's time to sound the alarm. If you're not being missed, maybe you're not needed. You need to kick it into a new gear and start producing more than you have been.

Scripture is clear: when we sharpen our skills, when we work with a spirit of excellence, we will stand before great men. Leaders will take notice. Promotion comes. Like cream rising to the top, you will rise higher as well. Remember, as you keep doing your best, as you stay faithful and keep growing, God will cause you to be noticed and move forward in the life of blessing He has prepared for you!

A Prayer for Today

Father, thank You for the gifts and talents You've given me. Help me to see the areas where I can rise higher. Help me to sharpen and improve my skills. I thank You for giving me favor and causing me to be noticed. I desire to serve diligently with an attitude of excellence so that I can bring You glory in everything that I do in Jesus' Name. Amen.

Wake-Up Thought

God wants to light a new fire under you. A person of excellence and integrity goes the extra mile to do what's right. He keeps his word even when it's difficult. People of excellence don't come in late, leave early, or call in sick when they are not. When you have an excellent spirit, it shows up in the quality of your work and the attitude with which you do it.

Get Your Fire Back

Today's Scripture

> *For this reason I remind you to fan into flame the gift of God, which is in you through the laying on of my hands.*
>
> 2 TIMOTHY 1:6 NIV

Have you ever wanted to do something really great? Maybe you had a big dream; maybe you believed you could start a business. Maybe you wanted to lose some weight or go back to school. Now, it's been so long. You tried and it didn't work out. The loan didn't go through. The medical report wasn't good. Now, the "never" lies are playing in your mind. *I'll never get well. I'll never get married. I'll never accomplish my dreams.*

Today is the day to get your fire back. Today is the day to get a new perspective. The Creator of the universe has already set the completion date for the dream He's placed in your heart. And just because it hasn't happened yet doesn't mean that it's not going to happen. God has already lined up the right people, the right breaks, the right answers. Everything you need is already in your future. Now you have to shake off the doubt; shake off the discouragement. Whether it's been a year, five years, or fifty years, whatever God promised you, He still has every intention of bringing it to pass. Keep standing, keep believing, keep hoping, and keep moving forward. Get your fire back and let Him fulfill every dream He has placed in your heart!

A Prayer for Today

*Father God, You are worthy to be praised.
Thank You for every dream and desire
You've placed within me. Today I choose to
press forward. I refuse to believe the "never"
lies. I believe You and choose to stand in
faith. Help me be diligent with everything
You have placed in my hand in Jesus' Name.
Amen.*

Wake-Up Thought

*Paul reminded Timothy to live with
enthusiasm. Do it with passion and some fire.
Give it your all. Don't settle for mediocrity.
Do everything with your whole heart. Stir
yourself up; rekindle that flame. Not only will
you feel better, but that fire will spread, and
soon other people will want what you have.
Wherever you are in life, make the most of it
and be the best you can be.*

Stay the Course

Today's Scripture

> *Whether you turn to the right or to the left, your ears will hear a voice behind you, saying, "This is the way; walk in it."*
>
> ISAIAH 30:21 NIV

God has put a promise inside each and every one of us. Oftentimes we have to go through the wilderness before we reach our promised land. Oftentimes, like Joseph, we feel as though we are in a pit long before we ever see the palace. Maybe you're in a season right now where you don't see anything happening. You think, *I've been praying and believing for a year, five years, ten years. It's not happening.*

No, be encouraged today. Stay the course. Keep believing. You may be tired, discouraged, and tempted to be frustrated, but don't give up on your future. Stay on the high road. Our God is a faithful God. It may be taking a long time, but what He started He will finish in your life. Scripture says the eyes of the Lord search to and fro to find someone who will be faithful on His behalf. Be the person He finds faithful. Keep believing, keep praying, keep obeying, and stay the course because He is leading you in the path of victory!

A Prayer for Today

Father, thank You for leading and guiding me in paths of righteousness for Your Name's sake. I choose to trust You even when I don't understand. I choose to believe that You are working behind the scenes for my good. I will stay the course and keep obeying You, knowing that You have blessing and victory in store for me in Jesus' Name. Amen.

Wake-Up Thought

If you will keep moving forward in faith, honoring God, you will come into a strength that you didn't have before, a force pushing you forward. That's finishing grace. When you could have gone under, God caused you to go over. When you could have been complaining, you had a song of praise. When you didn't see a way, He made a way. That's God breathing in your direction, helping you to become who He created you to be.

He Remembers You

Today's Scripture

> *Then God remembered Rachel; he listened to her and enabled her to conceive.*
>
> GENESIS 30:22 NIV

Our God is so loving, so merciful, so faithful. Even when we become too discouraged to believe, God does not forget what He promised. Maybe you feel discouraged today. Maybe your life hasn't turned out the way you had hoped. Maybe you prayed, believed, and worked hard, and it didn't work out. Now you're thinking, *Hey, I'm never going to be happy again. I'll never be married. I'll never accomplish my dreams.*

Remember today, not only does God remember you, but He remembers the promise He placed within you. He knows what He's destined you to do. You may have already said, "Forget it; it's never going to happen." The good news is that you don't have the final say. God has the final say, and He says, "What I started in your life, I'm going to finish." That dream you gave up on, God didn't give up on. He remembers you, and He is with you, leading you and guiding you to the place of victory.

A Prayer for Today

Father, thank You for Your faithfulness even when I am unfaithful. Thank You for drawing me close to You when I feel discouraged. Today I choose to lift up my eyes to You for You are my source of strength and help. I declare You are with me and guiding me to the place of victory. Fill me with Your joy by the Holy Spirit in Jesus' Name. Amen.

Wake-Up Thought

What God starts, He will finish. He is not okay with you partially fulfilling your destiny. God will make sure you complete what He put you here to do. You may not understand how it can happen. It may look as though you're too old, you missed too many opportunities, and it's no longer possible. But God has it all figured out. He knows how to connect the dots.

A Reason Isn't a Right

Today's Scripture

> *To all who mourn in Israel, he will give a crown of beauty for ashes, a joyous blessing instead of mourning, festive praise instead of despair. In their righteousness, they will be like great oaks that the LORD has planted for his own glory.*

ISAIAH 61:3 NLT

I t's easy to have a good attitude and pursue our dreams as long as everything is going our way. That doesn't take a lot of faith. But what about the difficult times—when a relationship doesn't work out, or you get a bad health report, or a friend does you wrong? It's easy to lose your passion when you're hurt. Too many people are sitting on the sidelines of life because they're injured. Now they're nursing their wounds, not moving forward because of what they've been through.

You may have a reason to feel sorry for yourself, but you don't have a right. God promised He will give you beauty for those ashes. He said He would pay you back double for the wrongs, but you have to do your part. If you're going to see the beauty, you have to shake off the ashes of self-pity. You have to shake off the discouragement and get back in the game. Every person has injuries. We all have wounds, but you can't let a loss, a health issue, a divorce, or a hurt be an excuse to sit on the sidelines. Today, get back in the game. Know that your best days are ahead. Know that He is working things together for your good, and He has victory in store for your future!

A Prayer for Today

Father, I praise You for Your love and compassion toward me. Today I choose to obey You and shake off the past. I shake off self-pity and discouragement. Help me to forgive those who have hurt me and begin to move forward into the good things You have in store for me. Thank You for giving me beauty for ashes and turning my sorrow into joy. I declare my best days are ahead in Jesus' name! Amen.

Wake-Up Thought

God wants to give you beauty for ashes, joy for mourning, and praise for despair. But here's the key: you have to let go of the ashes before God can give you the beauty. Ashes represent what's left over after something's been burned up—our broken dreams, our disappointments, our hurts, our failures. We all have our share of ashes, and God wants to give us beauty in exchange for them.

Forgetting What Is Behind

Today's Scripture

> *I do not count myself to have apprehended; but one thing I do, forgetting those things which are behind and reaching forward to those things which are ahead.*
>
> PHILIPPIANS 3:13 NKJV

We all go through disappointments, setbacks, and things that we don't understand. Maybe you prayed for a loved one, but they didn't get well. Or maybe you worked hard for a promotion, but you didn't get it. You stood in faith for a relationship, but it didn't work out. One of the best things you can do is release it. Let it go. Don't dwell on it anymore. If you go around wondering why things didn't work out, all that will lead to is bitterness, resentment, and self-pity. Before long, you'll be blaming others, blaming yourself, or even God. You may not understand what happened. It may not have been fair. But when you release it, it's an act of your faith. You're saying, "God, I trust You. I know You're in control. Even though it didn't work out my way, You said, 'All things are going to work together for my good.' So I believe You still have something good in my future."

There is power in letting go of the past and the frustration of trying to figure everything out. When you release your questions, you are saying, "God, You are in control. I trust You." And when you put your hope in God, that's when He can heal your heart and lead you forward into victory.

A Prayer for Today

Father, I love You and thank You for Your continued faithfulness in my life. Today I give You my hurts and questions. I release my frustrations and disappointments. I choose to trust You with my life even when I don't understand all things. Help me to forgive those who have hurt me and to let go of the past. Heal my heart and restore my soul. Show me the good plan You have for my future as I keep my mind fixed on You in Jesus' Name. Amen.

Wake-Up Thought

Adopt the Apostle Paul's attitude this morning. Shake off the ashes of yesterday's discouragements and disappointments and say to yourself, "I'm not looking back anymore at the mistreatment or the times when I got the short end of the stick. I'm not looking to the left or to the right. I'm looking straight ahead. I'm pressing forward, knowing God has good things in store for me."

Fix Your Mind

Today's Scripture

> *Whatever is true, whatever is noble, whatever is right, whatever is pure, whatever is lovely, whatever is admirable—if anything is excellent or praiseworthy—think about such things.*
>
> PHILIPPIANS 4:8 NIV

What you think about determines the quality and direction of your life. Naturally, people who think positive, uplifting thoughts have happier, healthier, longer lives. They are less stressed, more vibrant, and enjoy better sleep. That's why the Scripture encourages us to think on good things— things that are true, noble, and lovely. Some translations say to "fix your mind" on them. When you fix your mind on noble things, you close the door to the negative voices and open your heart to allow God to work in your life.

Choose today to fix your mind on good things. Do whatever you need to in order to keep those good thoughts before you. Write them on note cards and put them in a place where you can see them.

Confess God's promises over your life and declare His blessing on a daily basis. As you fix your mind on the goodness of God, you will rise higher in every area of your life. You will be filled with His peace and victory, and you'll see your dreams and desires come to pass.

A Prayer for Today

Father in Heaven, I praise You for Your mercy and grace. Today I close the door to negative thoughts and choose to fill my mind with Your Word. I choose to fix my mind on noble things, on things that are encouraging and uplifting. I will meditate on thoughts of peace and victory. Help me to guard my mind and thoughts throughout the day. Fill my heart with Your peace that I may glorify You in everything I do in Jesus' Name. Amen.

Wake-Up Thought

We must take responsibility for our minds and our actions. It's not your circumstances that get you down; your thoughts about your circumstances get you down. It is possible to be in one of the biggest battles for your life and still be filled with joy and peace and victory—if you simply learn how to choose the right thoughts. Fill your mind with God's Word.

Hope

Faith is the confidence that what we hope for will actually happen; it gives us assurance about things we cannot see.

HEBREWS 11:1 NLT

Something Better in Store

Today's Scripture

> *Because God had us in mind and had something better and greater in view for us...*
>
> HEBREWS 11:40 AMPC

Sometimes when things don't turn out the way you thought, or they don't happen on your timetable, it's easy to get discouraged and feel as though God has let you down. But that simply means that God has something better in store for you.

If you've been praying, obeying His commands, and standing in faith, but you didn't get the answer yet, now is not the time to back down. When one door closes, God always has another door.

We have to remember that the enemy is the one who is trying to bring discouragement. He's trying to get you focused on the closed door instead of the open door just ahead. Don't fall for the trap! Keep moving forward. Keep praising God in the hallway. Stay in faith, knowing that God has something better in store for you!

A Prayer for Today

Father, thank You for Your faithfulness in my life. I thank You for closed doors and open doors because You desire what is best for me. I am not going to focus on the negative circumstances, but on Your faithful promises. I trust You even when things don't turn out the way I had planned. I know that You are working behind the scenes and bringing something better into my life in Jesus' Name. Amen.

Wake-Up Thought

In the tough times, it's very tempting to continually talk about the problem, which only makes it bigger. Turn it around. Instead of complaining, "I didn't get the promotion," declare, "I know when one door closes that means God has something better. He's directing my steps. I'm excited about my future." Don't talk about the problem; talk about the promises of God.

Get the Capstone

Today's Scripture

> "Who are you, O great mountain? Before Zerubbabel you shall become a plain! And he shall bring forth the capstone with shouts of 'Grace, grace to it!'"
>
> ZECHARIAH 4:7 NKJV

In Scripture, when Zerubbabel wanted to rebuild the temple, he laid the foundation, but people came against him and forced him to stop. For ten years, no work could be done. The prophet Zechariah came by and told him to do something interesting. He said, "Go get the capstone." The capstone was the stone that was reserved as the final piece of stone for the building. It was symbolic. It represented the finished product.

Why was it important that he keep the capstone in front of him? Because every time he looked at it, it would remind him that God would finish what he started. When Zerubbabel was tempted to get tired and discouraged, he would go look at that capstone. That was God saying to him, "I'm still on the throne. I'm going to do what I promised. Just stay in faith."

Today, do you have your capstone in front of you? Do you have something that represents the final piece to your dreams? Keep that vision in front of you. Keep focused on where you are headed. Get the capstone and thank God for His faithfulness to complete the work in you.

A Prayer for Today

Father in Heaven, I praise Your holy Name. Thank You for the work You are doing in my life. Help me to keep the vision in front of me. I refuse to be discouraged because I know You are working in my life. I choose to keep my focus on You and Your unchanging Word. I desire to please You as I stay on the course You have set for me in Jesus' Name. Amen.

Wake-Up Thought

Is there something you see every day that reminds you of what you're believing for, something that inspires you, ignites your faith? Proverbs says, "Where there is no vision, the people perish." With no vision you'll get stuck. That's why many people have lost their passion. They don't have anything that reminds them of what they're dreaming about. Find something that represents the final piece to your dreams and keep it in front of you.

Promotion Comes from the Lord

Today's Scripture

> *For not from the east nor from the west nor from the south come promotion and lifting up. But God is the Judge! He puts down one and lifts up another.*

Psalm 75:6–7 AMPC

Have you ever noticed that people tend to act differently around those they think can do something for them—people who appear to have status, wealth, or influence in life? What if the way we treat people is a test. At times, God will bring people across your path who may seem insignificant. They may not appear to be able to do anything for you, but in reality, they are divinely linked to your destiny. They hold the key to your promotion and increase. Will you treat them with respect and honor even if you think they can't do anything for you?

The truth is, the people who we're playing up to or trying to win their favor may be the ones that will open a door for us. But they don't hold the key to your destiny. Promotion doesn't come from them. Promotion comes from God. And God will use the most unlikely people to open doors of opportunity for you—a hotel bellman, a maid, an intern, or an unpopular kid at school. Let's pass the test and treat everyone as though Jesus put them in our path because He probably did. Remember, God is watching and promotion comes from Him.

A Prayer for Today

Father, I love You and thank You for blessing my life. Thank You for ordering my steps, connecting me with the right people, and leading me on the right path. Help me to be a blessing and encouragement to people all around me. My desire is to honor and respect everyone, and in turn, I choose to honor You in Jesus' Name. Amen.

Wake-Up Thought

God has brought people into your life who are connected to your destiny. As you help them rise higher, you will rise higher. If you're too caught up in your own life to invest or to encourage them, you're going to get stuck. Reaching your highest potential is dependent on your helping someone else reach their potential. It's like a boomerang. When you help somebody else rise higher, it always comes back to you, and you'll rise higher.

Dig Deeper

Today's Scripture

> So let's not get tired of doing what is good. At just the right time we will reap a harvest of blessing if we don't give up.
>
> GALATIANS 6:9 NLT

Back in the 1800s some explorers were going across a huge desert and didn't bring enough water. They started digging at different spots underneath the surface about a foot or two, trying to find water. They ended up losing their lives in the desert because of a lack of water. Many years later, it was discovered that there was water right where they had lost their lives about three feet underground. If they would have just dug down a little bit farther, they would have found the water and saved their lives.

The same principle is true when you're in a dry season and not getting any good breaks, business is slow, or you're struggling in a relationship. It's easy to think, *This is never going to change. I'm never going to see my dreams come to pass.* No, just like those early explorers, water is there. Provision is there. You just have to dig down a little bit deeper. If you will shake off the self-pity, shake off what didn't work out, shake off the complacency, and turn up your praise, you'll soon tap into the blessing and provision He has prepared for you!

A Prayer for Today

*Father God, thank You for Your provision
and blessing in my life. I choose to praise and
worship You no matter what the circumstances.
I know that You are making a way even when I
don't see a way. Help me to stand strong in You
so that I may see the harvest of blessing You have
prepared for me. I declare that I am coming
into my due season in Jesus' Name. Amen.*

Wake-Up Thought

*This morning, you may be frustrated
because you feel God's plan isn't working in
your life. But never fear; God is arranging
all the pieces to come together to work out
His plan for your life. Don't grow impatient
and try to force doors to open in your own
strength. Your situation may look the same
as it has for the past ten years, but then one
day, God will bring it all together. When it's
your due season, God will bring it to pass.*

Don't Let the Storm In

Today's Scripture

Then He arose and rebuked the wind, and said to the sea, "Peace, be still!" And the wind ceased and there was a great calm.

MARK 4:39 NKJV

Have you ever thought about the fact that a boat can be surrounded by water, sailing through a vast ocean with water for miles in every direction, but it's not any problem unless the boat starts taking in the water? If the boat starts allowing the ocean to come inside, before long it will sink.

The same principle is true in life. You can have trouble all around you—stress, frustration, and worry. But the good news is, just like that boat, you don't have to allow what's on the outside to get on the inside.

When difficult times come, you don't have to be overwhelmed by the waves of worry or fear. Always remember, no matter what storms may come against you, the Creator of the universe lives on the inside of you. Speak peace to every area of your life, and don't let the storm in!

A Prayer for Today

Father, thank You for filling me with Your Holy Spirit and empowering me to stand against the storms of life. I will not allow the storm inside of me. I will remain at rest and at peace because You are fighting my battles for me. Today I declare peace over every area of my life and thank You for working things out for my good in Jesus' Name. Amen.

Wake-Up Thought

When an eagle faces a storm, he doesn't try to fight his way through the wind, through the rain, frustrated, struggling, putting forth all this effort. He simply stretches out his wings, and he lets the strong winds lift him higher and higher. Finally he rises above the storm, where it's as calm and peaceful as can be. Be like the eagle. Put your trust in God.

Refuse to Worry

Today's Scripture

> *"Can all your worries add a single moment to your life?"*
>
> MATTHEW 6:27 NLT

God doesn't want you to live worried and anxious about anything. He knows that worry is counterproductive. It steals your peace and joy and affects every area of your life—your sleep, your health, your peace. Worry steals precious moments of time that you can never get back.

Decide today to put an end to worry in your life. Don't feed worry by focusing on bad news all the time. Sure, we should be informed, but we should be more informed of the truth of the Word of God. Feed your faith by meditating on His Word and fill your heart and mind with God's promises. Declare every day, "My God shall supply all of my needs. He makes a way out of no way. He is my Restorer and Redeemer."

As you focus on God's Word, you'll drive out worry and fill your heart with faith and expectancy. You'll experience His peace and joy and move forward into the blessings God has in store for you!

A Prayer for Today

Heavenly Father, I praise and worship Your holy Name. I thank You that in Your presence is fullness of joy, peace, and rest. Today I choose to put an end to worry in my life. I choose to feed my faith by studying Your promises and declaring Your Word over my life. I declare that I will walk in Your supernatural peace no matter what the circumstances. Help me to totally trust in You today and always in Jesus' Name. Amen.

Wake-Up Thought

It takes the same amount of energy to worry as it does to believe. Why don't you take the same time you would normally be worrying and invest it in thanking God instead? Thank Him for working. Thank Him for the answer that's on its way. Thank Him for being in complete control. Instead of overanalyzing a bad situation, spend your time meditating on Scriptures such as, "God always causes me to triumph. I can do all things through Christ. I am strong in the Lord."

Believe and Enter Rest

Today's Scripture

> *Now we who have believed enter that rest.*
>
> HEBREWS 4:3 NIV

God desires for you to live in peace and rest no matter what is happening around you. When you believe God, you enter into His perfect rest. But if you are controlled by your circumstances, if you're up when things are up and down when things don't go your way, life is going to be a roller coaster. God's plan is for you to be stable, consistent, not moved by any of these things.

Anytime you face adversity or hit a tough time, one of the best things you can do is simply stay calm and keep your peace. When you're in peace, that's a position of power. You're saying with your actions, "God, I trust You. I know You are still on the throne. This may be difficult, but I know You are fighting my battles." That's what faith is—believing that God is who He says He is and that He is a rewarder of those who seek Him. When you believe God, you enter into rest and walk in peace and joy no matter what is happening around you.

A Prayer for Today

Father in Heaven, I worship You today because You are worthy to be praised. Thank You for Your peace and rest as I put my trust in You. Today I declare that You are my King, my Redeemer, my Healer, and my Deliverer! You are my faithful God! Help me to be consistent and steadfast, unmoved by the ups and downs of life. My faith and trust are in You, knowing that You have a good plan in store for my future in Jesus' Name. Amen.

Wake-Up Thought

When you live trusting God, you really don't have to struggle. You can be at peace, knowing that at the right time, God will keep His promise—and it's not going to be one second late. If you have some areas in your life in which you need to improve, you don't need to beat yourself up because you're not changing fast enough. When you are truly living by faith, you can relax in the "rest" of God. In total trust, you know He will bring it into being.

Be Still

Today's Scripture

> "Be still, and know that I am God."
>
> PSALM 46:10 NIV

When God created Adam, He put him in the Garden of Eden, a very quiet, peaceful, tranquil place. That's where God met him and spoke with him, in a place of peace.

Today's life can be very noisy. If we allow it, all of us can live stressed, uptight, in a hurry and on edge. In the midst of the whirlwind of activity going on around us, we have to learn to not let the busyness, the frustration and stress get on the inside of us. It may be hectic on the outside, but deep down in your spirit, you can be at rest because you know God has you in the palm of His hand.

Maybe you have been worried for a long time or stressed because a dream hasn't come to pass, or you're upset over a challenge you're dealing with. Just like God met Adam at a place of peace, God is saying, "There may be trouble all around, but I am calling you to a place of peace. Be still and know that I am God. Come to Me, and I will give you wisdom, strength, and grace for everything you face."

A Prayer for Today

Father, I love You and praise You for being the God of all peace. Help me to say no to the unnecessary activities that cause stress and frustration in my life. I want to draw closer to You and live in that place of peace. I choose to be still. I choose to find rest in You. I declare that I will walk in Your wisdom, strength, and grace for everything I face! I trust You, knowing that my days are ordered by You in Jesus' Name. Amen.

Wake-Up Thought

When things get busy, the children need you, it's hectic at the office, you have a thousand things to do, you have to put your foot down and say, "No, this is not an option. If I'm going to be strong, if I'm going to be my best today, if I'm going to have God's favor, I have to rearrange my priorities so I can spend time with God." When you invest in your spiritual well-being, it will pay huge dividends in your life.

Prewired to Be Imitators

Today's Scripture

> Therefore be imitators of God as dear children. And walk in love, as Christ also has loved us and given Himself for us, an offering and a sacrifice to God for a sweet-smelling aroma.
>
> EPHESIANS 5:1–2 NKJV

Have you ever spent time with a small child or baby and had them mimic your every sound or action? To them it's a fun game, but internally, they are learning by watching and copying everything you do. They just watch and do the same thing. That's because we are all prewired to be imitators.

Just like little children, we are all still imitators. So many people today end up imitating what they see in the world, on TV, in the news and magazines. But Scripture tells us that we are to be imitators of God and follow His example of love.

If you need to change your actions today, change what you are imitating by simply changing your focus. The more you focus on the Word, the more you will imitate God. And when you do things God's way, you will get God's results—peace, joy, and blessing all the days of your life!

A Prayer for Today

Father in Heaven, I thank You for Your goodness in my life. I choose to put You first place in my life and be an imitator of You. I set aside the things that are distracting me and put my focus on You and Your Word. I invite You to search my heart and mind. Give me Your heart of love and teach me to be an example of Your goodness in Jesus' Name. Amen.

Wake-Up Thought

This morning, believe you are made in the image of God. He created us in His image, and He is continually shaping us, conforming us to His character, helping us to become even more like the person He is. You are full of incredible potential. You have seeds of greatness. Love like Jesus, serve like Jesus, speak like Jesus, be like Jesus.

After This

Today's Scripture

> *And after this it came to pass that David smote the Philistines, and subdued them.*
>
> 2 Samuel 8:1 KJV

Your life is not over because you had a setback. God has an "after this" in your future. He has another victory planned. He wants to take you further than you ever dreamed possible!

When you go through tough times, don't be surprised if the enemy whispers in your ear, "You'll never be as happy as you used to be. You've seen your best days. This setback is the end of you." No, let that go in one ear and out the other. God is saying to you, "After the bad break, after the disappointment, after the pain, there is still a full life."

Know today that you have not danced your best dance. You have not laughed your best laugh. You have not dreamed your best dream. If you will stay in faith and not get bitter, God has an "after this" in your future. He's not only going to bring you out, He's going to bring you out better than you were before!

A Prayer for Today

Father God, I praise and worship Your holy Name. Thank You for the victory You have in store for my future. No matter what I have faced or am facing right now, I know there is an "after this." I declare that I am rising higher. I'm coming out stronger. I'm more prepared for my future. I'm better equipped and empowered to fulfill the destiny You have prepared for me in Jesus' Name. Amen.

Wake-Up Thought

The Scripture says Job went through all kinds of tough times. Everything was so bad that his wife told him, "Job, just give up. It's never going to get any better." But in the midst of that pain, Job said, "I know my Redeemer lives. I'm hurting, but my God is still on the throne." A year later, God not only brought him out of that challenge; God paid him back double for what he lost.

Be Devoted

Today's Scripture

> *Be devoted to one another in love. Honor one another above yourselves.*
>
> ROMANS 12:10 NIV

Being devoted to something means you are loyal to it by giving of your time, affection, and resources. What are you devoted to? Many people today are devoted to certain restaurants, television programs, and even their cell phones. And there's nothing wrong with any of that, but we have to examine our own hearts and see if we are being devoted to what God has called us to. Are you being devoted to the people God has placed in your life? Are you honoring others above yourself? The world's system says to "look out for number one—yourself," but God's system says to "look out for others, and I will look out for you."

Today, as you examine your own heart and life, ask the Lord to show you ways that you can honor others. One way is by being faithful to your word. Be a person of integrity and honor. As you live your life devoted to one another, you are honoring God. And He will repay you for your kindness and reward you in this life and in eternity!

A Prayer for Today

Father, I love You and praise You today. My desire is to live a life that is pleasing to You. Examine my heart and show me more ways I can honor You. Teach me to be a person of integrity and honor. Teach me to be devoted to others and be a blessing to those You bring across my path. Fill me with Your love and help me be an ambassador for You everywhere I go in Jesus' Name. Amen.

Wake-Up Thought

When David suffered unfairly at the hands of King Saul, he continued to treat Saul with respect and honor even if it involved suffering. It's easy to respect and honor others as long as they are being kind to us. But the true test comes when you get a "Saul" in your life, when somebody treats you unfairly for no apparent reason. If you will keep the right attitude, God will promote you at the proper time.

Faith Says "Thank You"

Today's Scripture

O give thanks to the Lord, for He is good; for His mercy and loving-kindness endure forever!

1 CHRONICLES 16:34 AMPC

When you live with an attitude of constant gratitude, not only will you thank God for what He's done in your life, you start thanking Him for what He will do in the future. You thank Him for opening doors for you. You thank Him for increasing you. You thank Him for bringing the right people into your life.

When we say "thank You" to God for the things that are coming, it's really a declaration of our faith in Him. It's saying, "God, I'm so sure of Your goodness, I'm so sure that You're working in my life that I'm going to thank

You right now for what You are going to do tomorrow." That's the kind of faith that pleases God. He wants us to trust in His goodness and believe that He is a Rewarder of those who diligently seek Him. He delights in seeing our faith. He delights in an attitude of gratitude.

Today, let your faith say "thank You." Praise Him throughout the day with an attitude of joy and expect to see His goodness in every area of your life!

A Prayer for Today

Father, thank You for another day to praise Your Name. Thank You for all You have done in my life and for what You will do tomorrow. You are a faithful Heavenly Father and I praise You with a grateful heart. Help me to keep an attitude of faith and praise no matter what the circumstances. I know You are a Rewarder of those who diligently seek You and that my future is bright as I serve and obey You in Jesus' Name. Amen.

Wake-Up Thought

Have you ever considered that perhaps you are not getting your prayers answered because you are not grateful for what God has already done for you?  *The Scriptures teach us that we should continually give God thanks; we should live with an attitude of gratitude. We have so much to be grateful for. We should get in the habit of giving God thanks all day long. Start by giving Him thanks for this new morning.*

Get Back Up Again

Today's Scripture

> *For though the righteous fall seven times, they rise again.*
>
> PROVERBS 24:16 NIV

Life is full of things that try to push us down. We all face disappointments and setbacks. Maybe you received some bad news about your health, or perhaps a relationship didn't work out. That was a setback. It's easy to get discouraged or lose your enthusiasm or even be tempted to just settle where you are. But if we're going to see God's best, we have to have a "bounce back" mentality. That means when you get knocked down, you don't stay down. You get back up again. You have to know that every time adversity comes against you, it's a setup for a comeback!

Remember, as a believer in Jesus, the same power that raised Christ from the dead lives on the inside of you. There is no challenge too difficult, no obstacle too high, no sickness, no disappointment, no person, nothing that can keep you from your God-given destiny. If you stay in faith, God will turn what was meant to be a stumbling block into a stepping-stone, and you'll move forward in strength, full of faith and victory!

A Prayer for Today

*Father God, I praise You for Your faithfulness.
I choose to get back up and move forward
today. I am not going to stay down because of
discouragement and disappointment. Thank
You for setting me up for success in everything
I do. I choose to trust and rely on You,
knowing that Your plans are for my good. I
know my best days are ahead of me and look
forward to the blessings You have in store for
me in Jesus' Name. Amen.*

Wake-Up Thought

*Do you know what made David king?
Goliath. God used the opposition to take
him to the throne. When you face great
difficulties, it's because God wants to take
you to your throne. He wants to take you to a
higher level. That giant is not there to defeat
you; it is there to promote you. You may be in
tough times, but the right perspective to have
is: I'm coming up stronger, better, increased,
promoted, and at a new level.*

Esteeming One Another

Today's Scripture

> *And walk in love, [esteeming and delighting in one another] as Christ loved us and gave Himself up for us, a slain offering and sacrifice to God [for you, so that it became] a sweet fragrance.*
>
> EPHESIANS 5:2 AMPC

We don't hear the word *esteem* very much in our culture, but the Bible tells us to esteem and delight in one another. One definition of esteem is "to hold in high regard." That means we are to honor and value one another and hold them in high regard, even if you don't always agree with them.

Sometimes people think, *That person doesn't act honorably, so why should I honor them?* But the truth is, we are to honor and esteem people because they are valuable in the eyes of God.

If you had a very costly and valuable piece of jewelry, you wouldn't just wear it to the gym or leave it on the kitchen sink. No, you would treat it carefully. You would put it in a safe place and protect it. It's the same way with people. When we see others as valuable the way God sees them, we treat them carefully. We speak respectfully. We look for the good in others and honor them for who God made them to be. Choose to esteem and delight in one another. Sow good seeds into your relationships and see a harvest of blessing in every area of your life!

A Prayer for Today

Heavenly Father, I honor and glorify You. Thank You for the people You have placed in my life. Today I choose to love and honor others. Help me to see the good and value in people. I want to esteem people and love them like You do. I know You have blessed me so I can be a blessing to people all around me. Help me to show Your love and kindness through my actions and words in Jesus' Name. Amen.

Wake-Up Thought

With some people, no matter what you do, it's not going to be enough, and they are not going to agree with you. But their happiness and approval are not your responsibility. Always be kind and respectful, and let your attitude be, You may be negative and do me wrong, but I will love and honor you. I choose to not be offended and upset. I'm not going to try to change things that I cannot change or to fix people who don't want to be fixed.

Magnify the Lord

Today's Scripture

> *O magnify the LORD with me, and let us exalt his name together.*
>
> PSALM 34:3 KJV

Something powerful happens inside when you magnify the Lord. What does it mean to magnify the Lord? When you magnify Him, you aren't changing Him; you are changing the way you see Him. You are making Him bigger in your life than your problems and circumstances.

So many people today waste time and energy talking about their problems and feeling sorry for themselves. That's because they are magnifying their circumstances in their own mind and heart. But when you start magnifying the Lord by talking about Him and worshiping Him, you are making Him the main priority in your life and opening the door for Him to move on your behalf.

Today, decide that no matter what's going on in life around you, you are going to magnify your God. Talk about His goodness. Talk about His faithfulness. Declare that He is working behind the scenes on your behalf.

A Prayer for Today

Heavenly Father, today I choose to magnify and exalt You. You are always faithful and good and worthy to be praised. I choose to focus on You and not the circumstances around me. I cast my burdens on You because You promised to sustain me. I know that You are bigger than anything I am facing today. Help me to keep my heart and mind focused on You all the days of my life in Jesus' Name. Amen.

Wake-Up Thought

You may have magnified a problem for so long, thinking about how it's never going to work out, making it bigger and bigger. But if you'll magnify your God, you'll see it from the right perspective; you'll realize it's nothing for God. All He has to do is breathe in your direction. The bigger you make God, the smaller your problems become, and the more faith will rise in your heart.

Talk Yourself into It

Today's Scripture

> *"You will also decree a thing, and it will be established for you; and light will shine on your ways."*
>
> JOB 22:28 NASB

In Genesis 17, when Sarah first heard the news that she was going to have a baby, the Scripture says it was so far out she began to laugh. She was in her nineties, so it seemed impossible from every angle. You can just hear her saying, "Abraham, a baby? Are you kidding? I've gone through the change of life. That defies the laws of nature." She was saying, "I'm at a disadvantage. I don't have what it takes." She was belittling herself, discounting herself. She was burying the promise deep within her.

When you think about it, it's just as easy to talk yourself into something as it is to talk yourself out of it. Instead of thinking of all the reasons why you can't get well, why you can't accomplish a dream, why your marriage is not going to last, and talking yourself out of it, start talking yourself into it! "I can do all things through Christ. God is making a way even though I don't see a way. I'm anointed, equipped, talented, more than a conqueror."

The more you speak God's Word, the more you believe it. When you believe God's Word, it comes to pass in your life. Start today by declaring His promises. Feed your faith and move forward into the victory and blessing He has in store for you!

A Prayer for Today

Father, thank You for Your continued faithfulness in my life. I choose to believe Your promises over the negative words and circumstances. You are a God who cannot lie. Even when it seems impossible, I know all things are possible with You. I choose to declare Your truth and talk myself into believing You instead of doubting. I declare I am anointed, equipped, talented, and more than a conqueror in Jesus' Name. Amen.

Wake-Up Thought

It's a simple truth that you cannot give birth to something you have not first conceived. You must conceive it on the inside through your eyes of faith before it will  *come to pass on the outside. We need to quit allowing our imaginations to keep us beaten down to where we don't think we can do anything. Instead, let's start allowing God to use our imaginations to build us up, to help us accomplish our dreams.*

Like Fire in Your Bones

Today's Scripture

"But His word was in my heart like a burning fire shut up in my bones; I was weary of holding it back, and I could not."

JEREMIAH 20:9 NKJV

In Scripture, God gave a promise to Jeremiah that he would become a great prophet and speak to the nations. But Jeremiah was young and afraid. He didn't see how it could happen. He started telling God all the reasons why it wouldn't work out. He said, "God, when I get up to speak, people mock me and make fun of me. I'm young. I'm tired. I'm intimidated." Just when you think he is going to talk himself out of it, he says, "Your Word was in my heart like a burning fire shut up in my bones." He was saying, "God, I may not see how it can happen. All the odds are against me, but this promise You put in me will not go away. It's like a fire. It's alive. I can't get away from it."

You may be at a place right now where you could easily give up on what God has placed in your heart. But like Jeremiah, there is a fire shut up in your bones. What God promised you will not die. You can try to ignore it. You can try to talk yourself out of it. Your mind may tell you that it's never going to happen, but deep down you feel a stirring, a burning, a restlessness. That's the promise God put in you. He loves you too much to let you be average. He is going to push you into greatness. Get ready because the gifts, the talents, the skills, the ideas, and the untapped potential are about to come forth!

A Prayer for Today

Father in Heaven, thank You for Your endless mercy. I may not feel qualified, but I know You are with me and equipping me for all good things. I declare that Your truth is like a fire shut up in my bones! I will speak it forth and see it come to pass! Help me to be strong and courageous. Help me to boldly embrace everything You have in store for me in Jesus' Name. Amen.

Wake-Up Thought

Our lives need to be inspired, infused, filled afresh with God's goodness and gifts every day. One of the main reasons we lose our enthusiasm in life is because we start to take for granted what God has done for us. Don't allow your relationship with Him to become stale or your appreciation for His goodness to become common. Don't take for granted the greatest gift of all that God has given you—Himself!

The End of Your Drought

Today's Scripture

> *You, O God, sent a plentiful rain.*
>
> PSALM 68:9 NKJV

Every person goes through times of drought, or dry seasons, when we don't see the changes we hoped for. We've got big dreams, we're standing on God's promises, but things stay the same. It's dry and barren. Maybe you are blessed in one area and in a drought in another. It's easy to think, *This is the way it's always going to be. I'll always have this struggle.* No, that drought is coming to an end. Any area of brokenness, dryness, loneliness, every empty place, if you will stay in faith, God is going to rain down favor, healing, and restoration.

Declare that today you are going to see an abundance of rain! Every drought is only temporary. That dry season is not going to last forever. Struggle and lack is not your destiny.

It's temporary. Rain is headed your way! Declare it by faith, "Father, thank You that the drought is ending and the rain is coming; and I will see an abundance of Your goodness in my life!"

A Prayer for Today

Father, I love You and honor You today. Thank You for Your refreshing rain on the dry places in my life. I know that what I am facing is temporary and the winds are shifting in my direction. Thank You for raining down provision, blessing, hope, wisdom, joy, and peace. Give me strength to stand strong in You as Your plan unfolds for my life. I declare that the drought is ending and the rain is coming; I will see an abundance of Your goodness in my life in Jesus' Name. Amen.

Wake-Up Thought

Constantly struggling, enduring, not having enough, and barely getting by are a drought. Do not accept that as your destiny. Jesus came that you might live an abundant life. We are to be the head and not the tail. And yes, we all go through dry seasons, but they are not permanent. They are temporary. At some point the drought will come to an end, and you will see an abundance of rain, an abundance of favor.

Choose Life and Blessing

Today's Scripture

> *"I call heaven and earth as witnesses today against you, that I have set before you life and death, blessing and cursing; therefore choose life, that both you and your descendants may live."*

DEUTERONOMY 30:19 NKJV

D id you know that with your words you can either bless your future or curse your future? Your words have creative power. If you want to know what your life is going to be like five years from now, just listen to what you're saying about yourself today!

Too many people go around saying, "I'll never get well." "I'll never get out of debt." "It's flu season. I'll probably get it." "This marriage is never going to last." Then they wonder why they don't see things turn around. It's because they're calling defeat into their future. They're calling in mediocrity. Don't let that be you!

When you get up in the morning, no matter how you feel, no matter what things look like, instead of using your words to describe your situation, use your words to change your situation. Make a declaration of faith by saying, "This is going to be a great day. I have God's favor. He's directing my steps." When you do that, you are choosing life and blessing. You are calling in favor, increase, and opportunities, and you will move forward in the life of blessing He has for you!

A Prayer for Today

Father, thank You for another day to praise You. I commit my words to You today. I know my words have creative power and I will use them to speak life and victory. I choose to speak good things over my life and bless my future. I declare this is going to be a great day. I have God's favor. You are directing my steps and You have a bright future for me in Jesus' Name. Amen.

Wake-Up Thought

Our words have tremendous power and are similar to seeds. By speaking them aloud, they are planted in our subconscious minds, take root, grow, and produce fruit of the same kind. Whether we speak positive or negative words, we will reap exactly what we sow. That's why we need to be extremely careful about what we think and say.

Hope

This hope is a strong
and trustworthy anchor
for our souls. It leads us
through the curtain into
God's inner sanctuary.

HEBREWS 6:19 NLT

Look Again

Today's Scripture

> *"Go and look toward the sea," he told his servant. And he went up and looked. "There is nothing there," he said. Seven times Elijah said, "Go back." The seventh time the servant reported, "A cloud as small as a man's hand is rising from the sea."*
>
> 1 KINGS 18:43–44 NIV

The Bible says that after the prophet Elijah prayed and asked God to end the drought, he said to the people, "I can hear the sound of an abundance of rain." He was saying in effect, "There is a yes from God in our future!"

Elijah told his assistant to go look on the other side of the mountain to see if there was any sign of rain. When the assistant came back, he said, "No, Elijah. There's not a cloud in the sky. It's perfectly clear." Elijah didn't get discouraged and think, *What are we going to do now? I might as well quit this prophet business.* No, he simply said, "Go back and look again."

This happened six different times, but Elijah kept saying, "Go look again." On the seventh time, the servant came back and said, "Elijah, I saw a small cloud in the sky. It isn't much, just the size of a man's hand." Elijah's answer was basically, "You'd better get your umbrella. Rain is coming!

Like Elijah, maybe you are believing for something, and you aren't seeing anything happen. Don't give up; go look again! If God has promised it, He will do it. It won't be long until you see His showers of blessing pouring down on every area of your life!

A Prayer for Today

Father, I love You and praise You for Your faithfulness in my life. I know there is a yes in my future. I believe that You are working behind the scenes even when I can't see it. I choose to focus on You and keep believing You and Your Word. I choose to look again until I see every promise fulfilled in Jesus' Name. Amen.

Wake-Up Thought

It may be a small yes, a faint yes, a barely-see-it yes, but when you're expecting things to change in your favor—when you know God has yes in your future—you will latch onto even a small sign by faith. "That's my yes.  *Other people may not see it. Other people may try to talk me out of it. Other people may say I'm just too positive, too hopeful. That's okay. I'm a believer and not a doubter. I know that's my yes."*

It's Never Too Late

Today's Scripture

> *The gifts and calling of God are without repentance.*
>
> ROMANS 11:29 KJV

What could be worse than to come to the end of life filled with regrets? "If only I had pursued that dream. If only I had been more disciplined. If only I had taken that step of faith. If only I had forgiven." Don't let that be you. You may have put things off a lot longer than you should have, but the good news is that it's not too late to get started. You can still become everything God has created you to be.

Today, make the decision to stop making excuses. If you always make excuses, you'll always have one. Don't wait for a more convenient time. It says in Ecclesiastes, "If we wait for all the conditions to be just right, we'll never move off of dead center." Make a decision to just do it! Be a now person. Your destiny is calling out, and it's never too late to be all that God has created you to be.

A Prayer for Today

*Father, I love You and praise Your holy
Name. I let go of all my excuses today and I
choose to trust You with my life and dreams.
Thank You for making all things new.
Thank You for renewing me, restoring me,
and setting me on the road to victory. Show
me Your ways and give me the strength to
embrace every opportunity that comes from
You in Jesus' Name. Amen.*

Wake-Up Thought

*Never put a question mark where God has
put a period. Quit living in a negative
frame of mind, stewing about something
that is over and done. Focus on what you
can change rather than what you cannot.
Shake yourself out of that "should have,
could have, would have" mentality, and
don't let the regrets of yesterday destroy the
dreams of tomorrow. It's time to get up and
get going. God has another plan for you.
And it is better than you can imagine!*

Through Faith and Patience

Today's Scripture

> Imitate those who through faith and patience inherit what has been promised.
>
> HEBREWS 6:12 NIV

In our culture today, people are used to getting things right away. Some people say that we live in a "microwave" society. In other words, we've been programmed for immediacy. People don't like to wait. But the Scripture says, "It's through faith and patience that we inherit God's promises."

Sometimes it's easy for people to start out in faith. We declare, "God, I believe I'm going to accomplish my dreams. God, I believe I'm going to overcome this obstacle." But it gets harder when we have to walk in patience. When you pray, you need to say, "God, I not only believe for big things but I trust Your timing. God, I'm not going to get discouraged if it doesn't happen immediately. I'm not going to give up because it's taken a week, a month, or five years. I know the set time is already in my future, so I'm going to wait with faith and patience because I know that it's on the way."

Remember, through faith and patience we inherit His promises. Trust His Word, trust His timing, and trust that your answer is on its way!

A Prayer for Today

Father, thank You for Your mercy and grace in my life. Help me to walk in faith and patience and trust Your perfect timing. I trust Your faithfulness. I trust Your goodness. I know that You are working things out in my favor and in Your timing. I declare that through faith and patience, I will inherit every promise You have for me in Jesus' Name! Amen.

Wake-Up Thought

If something is not happening on your timetable, remind yourself, "God knows what He is doing. He has my best interests at heart. I wouldn't be having this delay unless God has a very good reason for it." And while you're waiting, don't try to figure everything out. That's only going to frustrate you. Turn it over to God. Say with David, "God, my times are in Your hands. I know that at the set time everything You promised me will come to pass."

Victor's Mentality

Today's Scripture

> *No, in all these things we are more than conquerors through him who loved us.*
>
> ROMANS 8:37 NIV

In Scripture, Paul went through hard times. How did he come through? He wasn't complaining, living in self-pity or despair. No, he shook off that defeated mindset and chose to have a vision of victory. This is what we have to do, too!

Remember, you're not a weakling. You're not lacking. The most powerful force in the universe is breathing in your direction. Every morning you need to remind yourself, "I am ready for and equal to anything that comes my way. I am full of can-do power."

Listen, that sickness is no match for you. That relationship issue is not going to keep you from your destiny. The loss of that loved one did not stop God's plan for your life. Don't let it overwhelm you. You can handle it. You've been armed with strength! Keep a victor's mentality because a victor's mentality becomes a victor's reality!

A Prayer for Today

Father, I praise You for Your loving-kindness and mercy. Thank You for the victory that overcomes the world—my faith in Jesus Christ. I shake off a defeated mentality and expect victory because You are shifting things in my favor. Today I choose to trust You. I am full of can-do power because greater is He that is in me than he that is in the world! I stand on Your promises and choose to live with a victor's mentality in Jesus' Name! Amen.

Wake-Up Thought

God does not want to bring you out of your adversities simply as a survivor; you are "more than a conqueror." Notice that the Apostle Paul did not say we will become conquerors; he says we are more than conquerors right now. If you will start acting like it, talking like it, seeing yourself as more than a conqueror, you will live a prosperous and victorious life. The price has already been paid for you to have joy, peace, and happiness.

Daily Benefits

Today's Scripture

> *Blessed be the Lord, who daily loads us with benefits.*
>
> PSALM 68:19 NKJV

When you live a life that honors God, when you obey His Word and you're a person of excellence and integrity, the Scripture says that God's blessings will chase you down and overtake you. You won't be able to outrun the good things of God. He daily loads us with benefits!

People get confused sometimes and think they have to go chasing after the blessings. But really, when you chase after God each and every day, when you make Him your highest priority, the blessings will automatically follow.

Today make pleasing the Lord your top priority. Let go of anything that would hold you back or weigh you down. Be willing to deal with issues as God brings them to light. Don't give in to compromise and temptation that will keep you from God's best. Then get ready because His blessings will chase you down as He daily loads you with benefits!

A Prayer for Today

Father, I love You and I dedicate every area of my life to You today. I make pleasing You my top priority. Help me to live a life of integrity and honor. Help me to be strong to resist temptation and compromise. Thank You for daily loading me with benefits as I put You first in everything that I do in Jesus' Name. Amen.

Wake-Up Thought

This morning, instead of expecting to get the short end of the stick in life, why not start expecting God's blessings to chase after you? Instead of expecting to barely get by in life, start expecting the goodness of God to overtake you. Keep in mind that God has your best interests at heart, that He is working everything for your good. Like a good parent, He doesn't always give you what you want. But He always gives you what you need.

You Can Handle It!

Today's Scripture

> "Let him take hold of My strength,
> that he may make peace with Me."
>
> ISAIAH 27:5 NKJV

Isaiah said, "Take hold of His strength." When you make this declaration, "I can handle it," that's not just being positive. You're taking hold of strength. When you say it, you're getting stronger. That's why the Scripture says, "Let the weak say, 'I am strong.'" Don't be always talking about the problem, saying, "I can't stand this job." "This professor is so difficult. I'll never pass his course." "My loved one didn't make it. I don't know what I'm going to do." All that does is drain you. When you talk defeat, strength is leaving. Energy is leaving. Creativity is leaving. Don't let those things overwhelm you. You are not a victim; you are a victor!

No matter what comes your way, you can handle it! You are ready for it and equal to it. If you will stay in agreement with God, He will take what is meant for your harm and use it to your advantage. That difficulty won't defeat you. It will promote you into the life of blessing and victory He has in store for you!

A Prayer for Today

Father, thank You for Your grace and mercy in my life. Thank You for giving me the strength to handle anything that comes my way. I choose to speak positive words of faith, hope, and life over my life and circumstances. Whatever I go through, I can handle it because You always cause me to triumph in Christ Jesus! I love You and receive Your empowerment in every area of my life in Jesus' Name! Amen.

Wake-Up Thought

Colossians 3 says, "God has given us the power to endure whatever comes our way with a good attitude." Maybe someone has treated you unfairly. It's one thing to bad mouth the person. That doesn't take any faith. But if you want to pass the test, you have to take hold of God's strength and be good to people even when they're not being good to you. Every time you do the right thing, a blessing will follow.

Your Story Ends in Victory

Today's Scripture

> *You saw me before I was born. Every day of my life was recorded in your book. Every moment was laid out before a single day had passed.*

PSALM 139:16 NLT

In difficult times, you have to remind yourself that nothing is a surprise to Almighty God. He's not up in the heavens scratching His head, saying, "Oh, man, he got laid off. That messed up everything." "Oh, she was diagnosed with cancer." "Joseph was thrown into a pit." "Joel lost his father. Now what am I going to do?" No, God knows the end from the beginning. He has already written every day of your life in His book. The good news is that if you will stay in faith, your book ends in victory.

The next time you face an unexpected challenge, remember, it's no surprise to God.

He already has the answer, the provision, the healing you need. Keep standing, keep praying, keep hoping, and keep believing that your story isn't over until your story ends in Victory!

A Prayer for Today

Father, I praise and worship You today! Thank You for giving me the strength I need to overcome in every area of my life. You are a faithful God and You promised to sustain me. I know that You hold the days of my life in the palm of Your hand. I believe that You have equipped me with everything I need for spirit, soul, and body. I declare that I am strong in You and in the power of Your might in Jesus' Name. Amen.

Wake-Up Thought

The Scripture says, "Our faith is tried in the fire of affliction." When you're in a tough time, that's an opportunity to show God what you're made of. Anybody can become negative, bitter, and blame God. It's easy to lose your passion. But if you want to pass the test, if you want God to take you to a new level, you can't be a weakling. You have to be a warrior.

Don't Be Intimidated

Today's Scripture

> *Don't be intimidated in any way by your enemies.*
>
> PHILIPPIANS 1:28 NLT

With God on your side, there is no reason to be intimidated by your enemies. You don't have to be intimidated by cancer. It's no match for your God. Sickness cannot keep you from your destiny. God has you in the palm of His hand. Nothing can snatch you away. If it's not your time to go, you're not going to go. Don't be intimidated by that financial problem. Don't be intimidated by what somebody said about you. There is an anointing on your life that seals you, protects you, enables you, and empowers you. God has infused you with strength. The Scripture says that you can do all things through Christ.

Today, go out with confidence. Go out with boldness, knowing that if God is for you, it doesn't even matter who is against you! No foe can stand against the power of Almighty God. You are empowered and equipped for victory, so don't be intimidated!

A Prayer for Today

Father in Heaven, I give You all the praise today. Thank You for empowering me to live in victory no matter what I may be facing. I refuse to be intimidated because I know You are for me, in me, and with me. I am confident that no weapon formed against me shall prosper! No one or nothing can keep me from my destiny. I trust that no matter what comes my way, I am safe in the palm of Your hand in Jesus' Name! Amen!

Wake-Up Thought

No matter how big the enemy looks or how powerful it seems, there is a force in you that is more powerful than any opposition. Greater is He that is in you than anything that comes against you. Refuse to give up, refuse to fall into self-pity, refuse to let it overwhelm you. When you have this warrior mentality, this "I can handle it" attitude, all the forces of darkness cannot keep you from your destiny.

A Divine Shift

Today's Scripture

> The LORD makes firm the steps of the one who delights in him.
>
> PSALM 37:23 NIV

We know someone who never really liked his supervisor. Nobody at the company did. This supervisor was very hard to get along with and condescending. He had been a source of frustration year after year. It looked as though he could be at the company for twenty or thirty years. He kept a good attitude, but deep down he thought, *This is going to be a pain to put up with this guy.* One morning he got to work and the management had called a staff meeting. They told how this supervisor's wife got transferred to another state, and he had just resigned and was no longer with the company. What happened? A divine shift.

Suddenly, God changed things.

Today, you don't have to worry about the people who are trying to hold you back. God knows how to move the wrong people out of your life and bring the right people in. He knows how to get you to where you're supposed to be. Trust Him; trust His timing, because a divine shift is coming your way!

A Prayer for Today

Father God, I praise You for Your divine protection in my life. Thank You for making my steps firm. Thank You for shifting things in my favor. Bring the right people into my life and open the doors You have for me. I trust that You are ordering my steps and leading me into the good life You have prearranged for me in Jesus' Name! Amen.

Wake-Up Thought

God will not allow any person to keep you from your destiny. They may be bigger, stronger, or more powerful, but God knows how to shift things around and get you to where you're supposed to be. They may have been against you for years, but when God shifts things, they'll go out of their way to be good to you. Proverbs says God can turn the heart of a king. We may not be able to change people's minds, but God can.

His Plan Will Stand

Today's Scripture

> There are many plans in a man's heart, nevertheless the LORD's counsel—that will stand.
>
> PROVERBS 19:21 NKJV

God is strategic. He has laid out an exact plan for our lives right down to the smallest details. He knows the people you need to meet in order to fulfill your destiny. He knows who is going to give you a good break and who is going to put in a good word for you. He knows when someone is going to need to be there to help you out of a difficult time. God has it all figured out. He is not vague or approximate. He is orchestrating your life right down to the very second, causing you to be at the right place at the right time so you can meet the right people whom He has ordained before the foundation of the world.

You probably can look over your life and see how, time after time, God directed your steps to the exact moment. If you had been ten seconds earlier or ten seconds later, things would have played out differently. That's God orchestrating His plan. That's God ordering your steps. All you have to do is stay faithful to Him and follow His leading, because in the end, His plan will stand!

A Prayer for Today

Father, I praise and worship You today and give You all the glory. Thank You for Your goodness to me. You have always been faithful to me and I know You always will be. Thank You for orchestrating my life. I trust that my times are in Your hands. I trust that You are working things out for my good as I keep my faith and hope in You in Jesus' Name. Amen.

Wake-Up Thought

You can trust God's timing. What you're praying about and what you're believing for are not going to be one second late. If it hasn't happened yet, it doesn't mean God is mad at you. It doesn't mean it's never going to work out. God has already established the time down to the millisecond. You don't have to worry. Whether it takes twenty minutes or twenty years, you know that what God promised He will bring to pass.

Your Cup Runs Over

Today's Scripture

> *You prepare a table before me in the presence of my enemies. You anoint my head with oil; my cup overflows.*
>
> PSALM 23:5 NIV

God's dream for your life is that you would be blessed in such a way that you could be a blessing to others. David said, "My cup runs over." God is an overflow God. But here's the key: you can't go around thinking thoughts of lack, not enough, or struggle and expect to have abundance. If you've been under pressure for a long time and have difficulty making ends meet, it's easy to develop a limited mindset. *I'll never get out of this neighborhood. I'll never have enough to send my kids to college.* No, that may be where you are now, but that's not where you have to stay.

God is called El Shaddai, the God of More than Enough! Not the God of Barely Enough. Not the God of Just Help Me Make It Through. He's the God of Overflow!

Today, no matter what you may be experiencing, stir yourself up in faith and declare who God is in your life. Declare that He is well able; declare that He is more than enough! Declare that your cup runs over with the blessing and victory He has prepared for you!

A Prayer for Today

Father, thank You for Your grace, favor, and mercy to me. Thank You for being the God of More than Enough! You are the God of overflow! I know that You are preparing a place of blessing for me. I declare that my cup runs over with Your blessings in Jesus' Name. Amen.

Wake-Up Thought

Psalm 35 says, "Let them say continually, 'Let the Lord be magnified who takes pleasure in the prosperity of His children.'" It was to help them develop an abundant mentality. Your life is moving toward what you're constantly thinking about. If you're always thinking thoughts of lack, not enough, and struggle, you're moving toward the wrong things. All through the day, meditate on these thoughts: overflow, abundance, God takes pleasure in prospering me.

The Fullness of the Blessing

Today's Scripture

> *But I know that when I come to you, I shall come in the fullness of the blessing of the gospel of Christ.*
>
> ROMANS 15:29 NKJV

God's blessing is His supernatural empowerment. It is His favor. And we've all seen a measure of His blessing, but there is a whole new level He wants to take you to. God has promises and opportunities in store for you that you haven't even thought of yet! What you've seen in the past is only a fraction of what God wants to do in your future.

Understand that God likes to outdo Himself. He wants to open doors for you and bring out talents and abilities you didn't even know you had. Remember, the God we serve is a God of abundance. He is the God of more than enough. Not only does He want to meet your needs, He wants to give you enough to bless other people. That's living in the fullness of the blessing. Don't settle where you are. Your destiny is not determined by the economy, by your past, or what anyone else thinks or says. Your destiny is determined by Almighty God. He wants to overwhelm you with His goodness so you can walk in the fullness of the blessing!

A Prayer for Today

*Father, I love You and I come to You today
with an open and humble heart. Thank
You for Your supernatural empowerment in
my life. I ask You to bring out the gifts and
talents in me so that I can use them for You.
I desire to be a blessing to others. I declare
You are going to overwhelm me with Your
goodness and abundance and take me to a
higher level in Jesus' Name. Amen.*

Wake-Up Thought

*The Scripture says God will supply our
needs "according to His riches." So often we
look at our situations and think, I'll never
get ahead. But it's not according to what
you have; it's according to what He has.
The good news is that God owns it all. One
touch of God's favor can blast you out of
Barely Enough and put you into More Than
Enough.*

Is Anything Too Hard for Him?

Today's Scripture

> "I am the LORD, the God of all mankind. Is anything too hard for me?"
>
> JEREMIAH 32:27 NIV

A friend of ours has a son who got his driver's license a while back and really wanted a car. His father said to him, "Let's believe that God will give you a car." The son said, "Dad, God is not going to give me a car. You can buy me a car." He said, "No, let's pray."

They asked God to somehow make a way for the son to have a car. The young man had one in mind, but he would have been happy with anything. A couple of months later, this man's employer called him in and said, "For the last two years, we've made a mistake on your paycheck. We've been underpaying you." When they handed him the check for the back pay, it was $500 more than the price of the car the son had been hoping to buy.

The Scripture says, "Is there anything too hard for the Lord?" There is no telling what God will do if you'll dare to believe Him. Why don't you stretch your faith today? Give God something to work with. Declare His Word, meditate on His promises, and put Him first because nothing is too hard for Him!

A Prayer for Today

Father, I thank You for Your grace and goodness in my life. I know that with You, all things are possible! Nothing is too hard for You. I declare that You will supply all of my needs according to Your riches in Christ Jesus! I choose to stand in faith, I choose to trust You, and I choose to walk in every blessing You have in store for me in Jesus' Name. Amen.

Wake-Up Thought

It says in the book of Exodus, "I am bringing you out of lack into a good and spacious land." Not a small land. Not a little place. Tight. Crowded. God is bringing you into a land of plenty of room. A land that's running over with space. Running over with supplies. Running over with opportunity. If you're not in a spacious place, don't settle there. That is not your permanent address. It's only temporary. God is taking you to a good and a spacious land.

Today Is Your Day!

Today's Scripture

> This is the day the LORD has made; we will rejoice and be glad in it.

PSALM 118:24 NKJV

A lot of times, it can be easier to have faith for the future. We believe "one day" we'll get a good break. "One day" we'll feel better. "One day" the problem will turn around. If we're not careful, we're always putting our faith off, believing that in the future something good is going to happen. But true faith is always in the present. God is called "the Great I Am," not "the Great I Will Be." He wants to show you His goodness, His favor, and His mercy today!

If this is going to happen, you can't just have faith for the future. You have to believe that "today is my day." "This could be the day my health improves." "This could be the day I get the phone call I've been waiting for." "This could be the day my child comes back home." There has to be an expectancy that something good is going to happen. Not next week. Not next year. Not in the sweet by-and-by. No, expect that today is your day and watch what God will do in every area of your life!

A Prayer for Today

Father, thank You for another day to praise and serve You. I thank You that You are the great I Am! Thank You for Your hand of blessing, provision, guidance, hope, and love. I look for You to work on my behalf, and I praise You in advance for what You are going to do today. I declare that today is my day in Jesus' Name! Amen.

Wake-Up Thought

Average faith says, "Maybe one day I'll get out of this problem. I don't know. It's pretty bad." Uncommon faith says, "I know I'm not only coming out, I'm coming out better off than I was before." When you have uncommon faith, you don't just believe to make your monthly house payment. You believe to totally pay off your house. Uncommon faith is radical faith. It's extreme. You believe God can do anything.

Can God See Your Faith?

Today's Scripture

> *And when he saw their faith...*
> LUKE 5:20 KJV

Do you know what moves the hand of God? This may surprise you, but God is not moved by complaining and self-pity. He's not even moved by our needs. Yes, He is concerned about our needs; and yes, He wants to meet our needs, but we have to do our part and invite Him to work in our lives by exercising our faith.

When Jesus walked the earth, oftentimes right before He healed someone, the Bible says, "When He saw their faith..." Can God see your faith?

When God sees you doing everything you can to get well; when He sees you getting to work a little earlier because you really want that promotion; when He sees you bypass the cookie jar because you've been believing to lose weight; when He sees you bite your tongue to keep the peace in your house; when He sees you help others when you really need more help than they do; when God sees your faith, that's when extraordinary things will begin to happen. Faith opens the door for God to move. So demonstrate your faith today and watch the hand of God move in every area of your life!

A Prayer for Today

Father in Heaven, I love You and praise You. Thank You for placing faith in my heart. I choose today to exercise my faith and trust You. Help me to grow in faith as I read Your Word and stay close to You. Search my heart and show me anything that is displeasing to You. My desire is to please You in all I do in Jesus' Name. Amen.

Wake-Up Thought

The faith that Jesus "saw" was a paralyzed man being lowered into a room through the roof by four men who had carried him up on the roof. Other people in the room didn't get well who had the same opportunity. The difference was this man put actions behind his belief. God is looking for people who have faith that He can see. Not a faith that He can just hear, not a faith that just believes, but a faith that is demonstrated.

Don't Magnify Your Enemies

Today's Scripture

> "Who is this uncircumcised Philistine that he should defy the armies of the living God?"
>
> 1 SAMUEL 17:26 NIV

D id you know that when David faced Goliath, he never called him a giant? Other people did, but not David. He didn't brag on the enemy's power. He didn't magnify the obstacle. He did just the opposite. He called him an "uncircumcised Philistine." Not only did he not acknowledge who Goliath was or his strength, his power, and his experience, he took it one step further and diminished him. When he said, "He's an uncircumcised Philistine," he was saying, "This man is not in covenant with my God. He's not in covenant with Jehovah." In other words, "He doesn't have the favor on his life that's on my life. I know the favor of my God keeps my enemies from being able to defeat me."

So when he went to face Goliath, David said, "You come to me with a sword and shield, but I come in the Name of the Lord of hosts and this day the Lord will hand you over to me." How could David, a teenager practically half Goliath's size with no military experience, go out with such confidence and face Goliath, a skilled warrior wearing a full set of armor? It's because he understood this principle. David is the one who said, "The favor of God keeps my enemies from defeating me."

A Prayer for Today

Father, I praise You for Your presence in my life. Thank You for Your mighty protection and for empowering me to overcome every obstacle and adversity. I choose to magnify You over every negative circumstance. I declare that the favor of God keeps my enemies from defeating me! Thank You for paving the way to victory in every area of my life in Jesus' Name. Amen.

Wake-Up Thought

You may be like David, up against a big giant right now; a giant of debt, a giant of sickness, a giant of legal problems. It looks impossible in the natural. Do as David did—get a new perspective. There is no challenge too tough for you, no sickness too great, and no dream too far off. The same power that raised Christ from the dead lives on inside of you. The enemy would not be fighting you so hard if he didn't know God had something great in store.

Say of the Lord

Today's Scripture

> *I will say of the Lord, He is my Refuge and my Fortress, my God; on Him I lean and rely, and in Him I [confidently] trust!*
>
> PSALM 91:2 AMPC

Your words have tremendous power. No matter what you may be facing today, the words of your mouth can help set the course for your victory or set the course for defeat. You decide by what you say. When you wake up with an attitude of faith and expectancy and declare God's Word, you will be strengthened and empowered by His Spirit. But at the same time, if you go around talking about your problems or talking about defeat, it drains your faith and sets your focus in the wrong direction.

That's why it's so important today and every day to take inventory of what you are saying.

When challenges and obstacles arise, declare that God is your refuge and strength. Declare His Word. Declare that He is for you. Keep the weeds out of your heart by letting go of bitterness and choosing to forgive. Stay in step with God with your words and actions and receive His strength and power to be all He's called you to be.

A Prayer for Today

Father, I praise You and thank You for Your supernatural strength in my life. Thank You for Your Word that is refreshing water to my soul. I choose to have an attitude of faith and expectancy and to agree to say what You say about me. Strengthen me and help me focus on Your promises and not my problems. I declare I will speak faith and victory in Jesus' Name. Amen.

Wake-Up Thought

Psalm 91 says, "I will say of the Lord, He is my refuge and fortress." The next verse says, "He will deliver me, protect me, and cover me." Notice the connection. I will say and He will do. It doesn't say, "I believe He is my refuge and fortress." The psalmist went around declaring it: "He is my refuge and fortress." Notice what happened. God became his refuge and strength. God was saying in effect, "If you're bold enough to speak it, I'm bold enough to do it."

Now Faith

Today's Scripture

> Now faith is the substance of things hoped for, the evidence of things not seen.
>
> HEBREWS 11:1 KJV

Are you hungry for more of God in your life today? The Scripture tells us that faith opens the door for Him to move on our behalf. Faith is what pleases Him. It gives substance to the things we hope for and makes them tangible. We've all been given a measure of faith, but it's up to each of us to put it into action. Notice today's verse starts by saying, "Now faith." It's not "later" faith or "one day" faith. We have to have faith for today, right now.

Do you believe that God has blessings in store for you right now?

Do you believe He wants to pour out His favor on you today? When you step out in faith and declare His Word, you open the door to His abundant favor and blessing in every area of your life!

A Prayer for Today

Father God, I love You and give You all the praise and glory. Thank You for the gift of faith. I choose to believe Your Word, which is a lamp to my feet and a light to my path. I declare that I have now faith and that You are pouring out Your abundant favor on my life. Show me how to continue to grow in faith so I am pleasing You in every area of my life in Jesus' Name. Amen.

Wake-Up Thought

This morning, and every morning, you must choose to live with an attitude that expects good things to happen to you. Start your day with faith and set your mind in the right direction, then go out expecting the favor of God. Faith is what allows Him to do the impossible. Expect to excel in your career and rise above life's challenges. Believe God for a great future. You have good things coming!

Preferential Treatment

Today's Scripture

> His anger is but for a moment, His favor is for life.
>
> PSALM 30:5 NKJV

Most of the time we think, *Oh, God has bigger things to deal with than me. He's not interested in what's bothering me.* No, you are God's biggest deal. He wants to make you an example of His goodness. When you keep God first place, when you honor Him with your life, God puts something on you that causes you to stand out from the crowd; something that gives you an advantage. It causes good breaks and opportunities to be attracted to you. It's called the favor of God!

The word *favor* means "to assist, to provide with advantages, to receive preferential treatment." The favor of God will cause you to be promoted even though you weren't the most qualified. God's favor will cause your children to get the best teachers in school. It will help you find the best deals. It will put you at the right place at the right time. God is saying to you what He said to Abraham, "I'm going to assist you. I'm going to provide you with advantages. I'm going to cause you to receive preferential treatment." Believe it and receive it for today and all the days of your life!

A Prayer for Today

Father, thank You for Your goodness and faithfulness in my life. I believe and receive Your promises. I declare that I have Your favor, preferential treatment and advantages because Your hand of blessing is upon my life. I thank You that good breaks and opportunities are attracted to me! I trust that You are working behind the scenes and opening doors of favor in every area of my life in Jesus' Name. Amen.

Wake-Up Thought

To experience more of God's favor, you must first become more "favor-minded." To be favor-minded means that you expect God's special help simply on the basis that He is your Heavenly Father and He loves you. In no way should we ever be arrogant, thinking that we are better than somebody else, that everybody owes us something. But as God's children, we can live with confidence and boldness, expecting good things, because of whose we are.

Hope

We put our hope in the LORD. He is our help and our shield. In him our hearts rejoice, for we trust in his holy name. Let your unfailing love surround us, LORD, for our hope is in you alone.

PSALM 33:20–22 NLT

That You May Be Healed

Today's Scripture

> *Confess your sins to each other and pray for each other so that you may be healed. The earnest prayer of a righteous person has great power and produces wonderful results.*
>
> JAMES 5:16 NLT

Relationships are so important in the eyes of God. As His children, He desires that we live in unity and stay connected with one another. When we are transparent and pray for one another, something supernatural takes place. We open the door to God's abundant blessing and healing in our lives. When we walk in love and unity, our prayers become more effective, and His power is released in and through us.

Living in peace and unity doesn't mean you have to agree with everyone around you all the time. It means you look for common ground. It means you reach out to others; you pray for them and help meet their needs. When we put the needs of others first, God will make sure our own needs are abundantly supplied. Follow God's commands and pray for one another so that you may be healed!

A Prayer for Today

Father in Heaven, I praise and worship You today. Thank You for revealing Your truth to my heart. I choose to obey Your Word. Help me to be sensitive to others and show me how I can pray and be a blessing to them. I choose to pray for others and live in peace and unity, knowing that it will open the door for Your healing in Jesus' Name. Amen.

Wake-Up Thought

Scripture instructs us to put on a fresh new attitude every morning, especially in our family relationships. Don't let little things build up. Don't harbor unforgiveness and resentment. Don't allow bad attitudes to develop, even those that may seem insignificant to you, because over time that bitter attitude will build and disrupt your peace and unity. Do your best to keep your own heart free and clean, or eventually anger and bitterness will show up and affect your relationships.

Don't Settle for Good Enough

Today's Scripture

> *For this reason I remind you to fan into flame the gift of God, which is in you.*
>
> 2 TIMOTHY 1:6 NIV

Too many people today have settled for "good enough." They've lost their passion and just sort of go through the motions of everyday life. At one time, they had a big dream. They were excited about the future, but they hit some bumps along the way. Something didn't happen on their timetable. Now they've gotten discouraged, thinking that it's never going to happen. They accept it as their lot in life.

Don't let that be you! Just because you haven't yet seen what God promised come to pass doesn't mean that it's not going to happen. Don't make the mistake of settling for good enough! Good enough is not your destiny.

You are a child of the Most High God. You have seeds of greatness on the inside. You were created to excel, to live an abundant life! It's not over until God says it's over. Start believing again. Start dreaming again. Start pursuing what God put in your heart. Stir up the fire within you and don't settle for good enough!

A Prayer for Today

Father, I praise You for Your mercy and goodness in my life. Today I declare that I will not settle for good enough. I refuse to be discouraged and give up on my dreams because Your timetable is perfect. I will stir up the dreams, passion, and flame within me. Lead me in Your path of truth as I press on toward the promises You have in store for me in Jesus' Name! Amen.

Wake-Up Thought

The good news is that just because you gave up on a dream doesn't mean God gave up. You may have changed your mind, but God didn't change His mind. He still has a victorious plan in front of you. What God spoke over your life, what He promised you in the night, what He whispered in your spirit, those hidden dreams, He will bring to pass. Why don't you get in agreement with Him?

Go All the Way!

Today's Scripture

> The LORD had said to Abram, "Go from your country, your people and your father's household to the land I will show you."
>
> GENESIS 12:1 NIV

In the Scripture, Abraham is listed as one of the heroes of faith. God made one of the first covenants with him. But what's interesting is that before Abraham, God spoke to Abraham's father and told him to go where he also told Abraham to go. It says in Genesis that Abraham's father "left Ur and headed out toward Canaan." He was going to the Promised Land just as God told Abraham. But it says, "He stopped along the way and settled in Haran." Why did he stop? There were too many difficulties. It was hard traveling with all of his flocks and herds. He had his family, his possessions. It wasn't comfortable. He finally decided, "I can't go any farther. I know this isn't the Promised Land, but it's good enough."

How many times do we do the same thing? We start off right. We've got a big dream. We're going to fulfill our destiny. But along the way, we face opposition. Adversity arises. Too many times, we say like Abraham's father, "What's the use? I'm just going to settle here. It's good enough." No, light a new fire in you. Decide today: "I'm not going to settle halfway, three-fourths of the way, or nine-tenths of the way. I'm going to make it all the way into my promised land."

A Prayer for Today

Father, thank You for Your supernatural direction in my life. Today I declare that I won't settle for good enough. I won't settle halfway to Your promises. Even though adversity and opposition arise, I choose to stand strong, dig my heels in, and press forward into the promised land you have prepared for me. I declare I am going all the way in Jesus' Name. Amen.

Wake-Up Thought

Maybe like Abraham's father you've already settled halfway, and you've gotten comfortable in that spot where you are. Challenge yourself to pull up your stakes, pack your tents, get your belongings, and start moving forward. Enlarge your vision! You may have had a delay, but you can begin again this very day. You simply need to focus on your goal, set your course, and declare, "I'm going to reach my full potential in God."

A Thousand Times More

Today's Scripture

> "May the LORD, the God of your ancestors, increase you a thousand times and bless you as he has promised!"
>
> DEUTERONOMY 1:11 NIV

This is our prayer for you today—that God will bless you a thousand times more than you are. Can you receive that into your spirit? A thousand times more favor...a thousand times more resources...a thousand times more strength?

Most of the time our thinking goes, *TILT! TILT! TILT!* because we've had the wrong mentality for too long. We've lived in the land of "not enough," and we haven't even explored the land of "a thousand times more." But today, why don't you get a new vision for your future? Why don't you dare to believe that God is about to increase you? Why don't you get up every morning and say, "Lord, I want to thank You that You are opening up the heavens, raining down favor, lavishing me with good things"?

If you'll have an abundant mentality, it won't be long before you'll see an abundant reality! Dare to believe that God wants to bless you a thousand times more!

A Prayer for Today

Father, I praise You for Your goodness and faithfulness in my life. Thank You for choosing to bless and increase me a thousand times more. I declare that I will have an abundant mentality, and I dare to believe for increase in every area of my life! I choose to open my heart and mind to receive everything You have in store for me in Jesus' Name. Amen.

Wake-Up Thought

David, who is called "a man after God's own heart," left billions of dollars for his son to build God's temple. Get rid of the thinking that, God wouldn't want me to have too much. That wouldn't be right. It's just the opposite. When you have an abundant mentality and a desire to advance the kingdom, God will open up the doors of His sky vaults to where you not only accomplish your dreams, but you can help be a blessing to the world.

Don't Let Others Control You

Today's Scripture

> *It is an honor for a man to cease from strife and keep aloof from it, but every fool will quarrel.*

PROVERBS 20:3 AMPC

Did you know that when you allow someone else's words or actions to upset you, you're allowing them to control you? When you say, "You make me so mad," you're really just admitting that their actions have power over you. As long as that person knows they can push your buttons, as long as you keep responding the same way, you are giving them exactly what they want. Sure, people have a right to say and do things that are upsetting, but we also have a right to not get offended. We have a right to overlook their actions. In fact, the Bible says that it's an honor for a man to keep "aloof" from strife. In other words, we have to remove ourselves, either physically or emotionally, from strife and offense. It's not easy, but we can choose to let it roll off of us like water off a duck's back!

Remember, you don't need everyone to agree with you all the time. You don't have to have the approval of others in order to be approved by God. Your job is to be the person God made you to be. Overlook offenses and let go of strife so you can live in peace and victory all the days of your life!

A Prayer for Today

Father, thank You for loving, accepting, and approving of me just as I am. I refuse to allow people and circumstances to keep me upset and steal my joy and faith! I know You are doing a work in my life, and I ask for the strength and confidence to overlook offenses so that I can honor You in everything I do. I declare the joy of the Lord is my strength in Jesus' Name. Amen.

Wake-Up Thought

Don't allow circumstances in your life or what other people say and do upset you. Don't give your power away. Exercise your right to be calm and peaceful and not let it ruin your day. Rise above every difficulty, knowing that God has given you the power to remain calm. Choose to live your life happy, ignore the offense, and let God fight your battles.

Handling Adversity

Today's Scripture

> *We can rejoice, too, when we run into problems and trials, for we know that they help us develop endurance. And endurance develops strength of character, and character strengthens our confident hope of salvation.*
>
> ROMANS 5:3–4 NLT

The way you handle adversities has a huge impact on your success in life. If you shrink back, choose to get bitter, and lose your enthusiasm, you are allowing the difficulties of life to bury you. You are allowing hardship to keep you from your God-given destiny. But if you choose to keep pressing forward with a smile on your face, rejoicing even in the hard times, you are allowing God's character to be developed inside of you. You are setting yourself up for promotion.

Think about this: the only difference between a piece of black coal and a priceless diamond is the amount of pressure that it's endured. When you stand strong in the midst of the trials and difficulties in life, when you allow God to shape and mold your character, it's like going from a piece of coal to a priceless diamond. Those difficulties are going to give way to new growth, new potential, new talent, new friendships, new opportunities, new vision. You're going to see your life blossom in ways that you've never even dreamed!

A Prayer for Today

Father in Heaven, I praise You for Your continued faithfulness in my life. Thank You for giving me strength to overcome every obstacle in life. I declare that I will press forward with a smile on my face and allow Your character to  *be developed inside of me. You are setting me up for promotion! I choose to rejoice no matter what may come against me. I know You are working all things together for my good in Jesus' Name! Amen.*

Wake-Up Thought

The tough times of life cause us to grow; that's when our faith is stretched. Your faith is similar to a muscle. It grows stronger through resistance. It is exercised when it's being stretched, when it's being pushed. That's why God does not usually deliver us from adversity overnight. He doesn't remove us from every uncomfortable situation in a split second. He uses those times to build our "spiritual muscles."

Press Past the Mountain

Today's Scripture

> The LORD our God said to us at Horeb, "You have stayed long enough at this mountain."
>
> DEUTERONOMY 1:6 NIV

Have you been facing a mountain for so long that you feel as though you are just sort of stuck there? Maybe at one time you knew you would break that addiction. You knew you would beat that sickness. You knew you would get married. But you've gone through disappointments. It didn't happen the way you thought.

Today, God is saying to you what He said to the people of Israel. "You have dwelt long enough on this mountain." It's time to move forward. God has new levels in front of you, new opportunities, new relationships, promotions, breakthroughs. But you have to stir up your fire. You have to get a vision for victory.

The dreams, the promises that you've pushed down and thought, *Oh, it's not going to happen. I'm too old. I don't have the connections. I don't know the right people,* God has it all figured out. If you will start believing again, start dreaming again, start pursuing what God put in your heart, God will make a way where you don't see a way. Press past the mountain and move forward into victory!

A Prayer for Today

Father, thank You for Your grace and mercy on my life. Thank You for empowering me to overcome every obstacle and press past every mountain. I choose to start dreaming again! I know You will make a way where there is no way! Help me move forward from this moment on. I look to You to lead and guide me into victory in every area of my life in Jesus' Name. Amen!

Wake-Up Thought

Don't you dare settle for second best. Don't get stuck in a rut thinking that you've reached your limits. Draw the line in the sand and say, "That's it. I'm stirring up the fire. Today is a new day. My dream may not have happened yet, but I'm not settling. I'm stretching my faith, looking for opportunities, taking steps to improve. I'm going to become everything God has created me to be."

Keep Faith Alive

Today's Scripture

> *No unbelief or distrust made him waver (doubtingly question) concerning the promise of God, but he grew strong and was empowered by faith as he gave praise and glory to God.*
>
> ROMANS 4:20 AMPC

Scripture tells us that faith without works is dead. In other words, if the faith inside of us doesn't get expression through our actions and words, it will no longer be alive. If we don't use it, we will lose it, so to speak. We have to step out in faith in order to keep faith alive.

Every person has been given a measure of faith by God. When we hear the truth of God's Word, we receive more faith. That's why it's so important to put the Word of God inside of you, because when you do, you are building your faith. To keep that faith alive and thriving, you have to put it to use. One way to put your faith into action is through praise and worship. Praise is a supernatural force that causes you to stand strong in faith even when your thoughts or circumstances are coming against the truth. Praise keeps your thoughts going in the right direction. It's hard to be negative when you are declaring the goodness of God!

Today, let praise make you stable and strong. Put that faith in your heart into action. Look for reasons to thank God. As you do, you'll feel that inner strength and be empowered to move forward into victory all the days of your life.

A Prayer for Today

Father, I praise You for life and health.
Thank You for provision, healing, strength,
and joy. I choose to make Your Word a
priority in my life and grow in faith daily.
Give me wisdom and revelation to know
You more. I choose to praise You at all times
no matter what the circumstances. Today
I put my faith in action by praising You
throughout the day in Jesus' Name. Amen.

Wake-Up Thought

You may be sitting
around waiting for
God to change your
circumstances. Then you
will be happy; then you
will have a good attitude; then you will give
God praise. But God is waiting on you to
get up on the inside and give Him praise
for all He has done now. When you do your
part, He'll begin to change things and work
supernaturally in your life.

In His Hand

Today's Scripture

> *Fear not [there is nothing to fear],*
> *for I am with you; do not look around*
> *you in terror and be dismayed, for I*
> *am your God. I will strengthen and*
> *harden you to difficulties, yes, I will*
> *help you; yes, I will hold you up and*
> *retain you with My [victorious] right*
> *hand of rightness and justice.*

ISAIAH 41:10 AMPC

We all face situations in life that feel out of control. During times like these, it's easy to get discouraged and allow fear to creep in. But instead, focus on the fact that God is holding you in the palm of His hand. There is nothing too difficult for Him; nothing is impossible, nothing is beyond His ability. When God holds you in His hand, you are safe. You are cared for. In His hand, there is victory. In His hand, there is strength. In His hand, there is provision. In His hand is everything you need!

No matter what you may be going through today, you can trust that God is for you. Instead of getting down and depressed over your circumstances, look up and get a vision of God turning that situation around. Let faith arise in your heart and focus on His favor, promotion, and blessing. See yourself in the palm of His hand, and see the victory and blessing He has prepared for you!

A Prayer for Today

Father, thank You for Your loving care in my life. I take comfort in the fact that You hold me in the palm of Your hand. You are helping me and holding me in Your victorious right hand. I choose to trust You even when things don't make sense, even when things seem beyond my control. I declare You are turning my situation around! I release my cares to You, knowing that You work all things together for my good in Jesus' Name. Amen.

Wake-Up Thought

When it looks impossible, when all the odds are against you, when it seems permanent, remember that the Creator of the universe has you in the palm of His hand. God is saying, "This is your time. Today is your moment. Get ready for release. Get ready for a breakthrough. Get ready for healing. Get ready for increase." Chose to believe even when it looks impossible.

Freedom in Contentment

Today's Scripture

> *I have learned to be content whatever the circumstances.*
>
> PHILIPPIANS 4:11 NIV

In life, sometimes it's easy to get so focused on our dreams and goals that we tune out everything else. We can get to the point where we're not going to be happy until we see those things happen. If we have to have something in order to be happy, our lives will be out of balance. When our goals and dreams start to frustrate us, and we lose our peace and don't enjoy life, that's a clear sign that we're holding on too tightly. What's the solution? You have to release it. Freedom comes when you say, "God, I'm turning it all over to You. You know my desires and what's best for me. I'm choosing to trust You and Your timing."

When we learn to be content whatever the circumstances, it takes away the power of the enemy. It takes away his ability to frustrate us. Not only that, but by our actions, we are showing our faith in God. When you choose to trust His timing, you can live in peace, you can live in joy, and you can rest in Him, knowing that He has good things in store for your future. Today, find freedom in contentment and rest in His everlasting peace.

A Prayer for Today

Father God, thank You for Your faithfulness. Today I choose to trust You. I release frustration over the dreams and desires in my heart because You know what's best for me. My times are in Your hands. Help me walk in peace and contentment no matter what the circumstances. I choose to trust Your loving care for me, knowing that You are faithful. I will bless You in all things in Jesus' Name. Amen.

Wake-Up Thought

Don't miss a great season in your life wishing you had more, complaining about what you don't have. The real joy in  *life is in finding contentment in the simple things—making memories with your family, watching a movie together, playing hide-and-seek in the house, enjoying the sunset, and staring up at the stars at night with your spouse. Learn to enjoy the simple things in life.*

Freedom for All

Today's Scripture

> "God does not show favoritism but accepts from every nation the one who fears him and does what is right."
>
> ACTS 10:34–35 NIV

Where the Spirit of the Lord is, there is freedom! And God's freedom is free for everyone. It doesn't matter what your nationality or heritage or who your family is. It doesn't matter how much money you have or don't have. God wants you free from everything that would hold you back in this life. He wants to pour out His blessing on all who honor Him and choose His ways.

It says in Galatians that in Christ there is no Jew or Greek or even male or female. That means God's not judging you based on physical conditions; He's looking at your heart.

He's looking at the gifts He's placed inside of you.

Don't let the enemy lie to you and tell you that God is blessing everyone else but you. Look for the ways He is pouring out blessing in your life. Thank Him for His acceptance, love, and freedom today. Focus on honoring Him and doing what is right. Receive His favor and blessing because it is a free gift for all!

A Prayer for Today

Father, thank You for loving and accepting me today. Thank You for Your freedom. I choose to honor You with my attitude, words, and actions. Point out in me anything that I need to change or improve. Show me how to live as an example of Your goodness all the days of my life. Thank You that whomever the Son sets free is free indeed in Jesus' Name! Amen.

Wake-Up Thought

Too often we're announcing and declaring the wrong things. "Prices are so high. Work is slow. Everyone else is getting good breaks." That's announcing you don't believe God is blessing you. You have to change what's coming out of your mouth. Start boldly declaring, "I am free. I am healthy. I am blessed. I am victorious. God's favor is coming—breakthroughs, healing, and promotions are on the way."

When You Feel Buried

Today's Scripture

> *"Most assuredly, I say to you, unless a grain of wheat falls into the ground and dies, it remains alone; but if it dies, it produces much grain."*
>
> JOHN 12:24 NKJV

We all face difficulties and challenges in life. But you have to remember, as a believer in Jesus, you have the life-giving seed of Almighty God on the inside of you. When you go through disappointments or tough times, you may feel as though you've been buried. You may feel as though you're in a dark, lonely place. You may feel like it's the end; but in reality, it's only the beginning. The fact is, you haven't been buried; you have been planted. That means you're coming back. And not only are you coming back, but you're coming back in increase, better and stronger than before!

In those tough times, you have to draw the line in the sand. Make a declaration, "This difficulty is not going to bury me. This loss, this disappointment, this injustice is not going to cause me to give up on my dreams. I refuse to live in self-pity. I know I am a seed. That means I cannot be buried. I can only be planted. I may be down, but it's only temporary. I know I'm not only coming back, but I'm coming back even better than I was before!"

A Prayer for Today

Father in Heaven, I love You and praise You today. Thank You for filling me with Your life-giving seed. I choose today to focus on the potential for my future. I may have gone through a setback, but I declare I will have a comeback! I am increasing and growing stronger and better! I know that I will overcome every obstacle by Your power that is at work in me in Jesus' Name. Amen.

Wake-Up Thought

It says in the book of Exodus, "The more opposition, the more they increased." When you feel you're in a dark, lonely place, don't get depressed and say, "God, why is this happening to me?" Your attitude should be: I know this opposition is a sign that increase is headed my way. It looks like a setback, but I know it's really a setup. It will not be a stumbling block to take me down. God will use it as a stepping-stone to take me up.

A New Season of Goodness

Today's Scripture

> The tongue can bring death or life.
>
> PROVERBS 18:21 NLT

God wants to do new and incredible things in your life! He has a new season of goodness in store for you today. The power to see His plan come to pass in your life is found in the power of your words. When you get in agreement with God, when you say what He says, that's when things will change in your life.

Life and death are in the power of the tongue. No one else chooses your words but you! You can speak forth seeds of life or seeds of death. What you have in your life today is a direct result of your words in the past, and what you will see in the future is a direct result of what you are speaking today.

Why don't you choose to bless your future? Why don't you choose to declare that it's a new season? Choose to speak what God speaks and believe that He has a new season of goodness in store for you today!

A Prayer for Today

Father God, I love You and thank You for Your goodness. Today I choose to speak words of life over myself and my future. I know that You have a good plan for me and I am in agreement with that plan. I speak blessings over my life. I declare this is a new season; it's a new day, and Your goodness and blessing are coming my way in Jesus' Name! Amen.

Wake-Up Thought

The Bible compares the tongue to the small rudder of a huge ship, which controls the ship's direction. Similarly, your tongue will control the direction of your life. You create an environment for either good or evil with your words, and if you're always murmuring, complaining, and talking about how bad life is treating you, you're going to live in a pretty miserable world. Use your words to change your negative situations and fill them with life.

A Rainstorm Is Coming

Today's Scripture

> Then Elijah said to Ahab, "Go get something to eat and drink, for I hear a mighty rainstorm coming!"
>
> 1 KINGS 18:41 NLT

In 1 Kings 18, the Samaritans had been in a great famine. For three and a half years, there had been no rain. The prophet Elijah showed up and said to King Ahab, "I hear the sound of the abundance of rain." When he said that, there wasn't a cloud in the sky, yet he chose to believe what he heard in his spirit in spite of what he saw in the natural. With his eyes, he saw drought, famine, and barrenness; but inside, he heard the sound of the abundance of rain.

This is what faith is all about. You have to believe what you hear in your heart even when you see just the opposite. God is saying,

"There's about to be an abundance of favor in your life. The drought is coming to an end. You're going to see healing, restoration, new opportunities, new growth."

Soon after, that rainstorm came. And just like Elijah, you have to believe that your rainstorm of blessing is right around the corner. No matter what anyone says, no matter what happens, keep believing and keep declaring because soon you will hear the sound of rain!

A Prayer for Today

Father in Heaven, I praise You for You are the Almighty God. Thank You that You are a God of abundance and You desire to bless and help me. I declare that the drought is coming to an end and an abundance of rain is coming my way! Thank You for the blessing and victory You have in store for my future. Help me to see and hear in my heart the good things You have planned. I choose to keep my eyes on You and declare Your blessing over my life in Jesus' Name. Amen.

Wake-Up Thought

Elijah sent his assistant seven times to look on the other side of the mountain to see if there was any sign of rain before the answer came. Had Elijah given up on the first no or the sixth no, it would have never happened. Think about this. When Elijah sent his assistant out to look, that was an act of his faith. Faith is what causes God to move. There are yeses in your future waiting for you to go looking for them.

God's Dream for Your Life

Today's Scripture

> *"My thoughts are nothing like your thoughts," says the LORD. "And my ways are far beyond anything you could imagine."*
>
> ISAIAH 55:8 NLT

We all have dreams and goals. We do our best to stretch our faith and believe that one day, if we work hard enough, get the right breaks, or meet the right people, we'll see that dream come to pass. In our mind, that would be big—a great accomplishment. But what's big to us is not big to God. He created the universe. He spoke worlds into existence. God's dream for your life is so much bigger than your own.

See, we think ordinary; God thinks extraordinary!

Today, whatever you're dreaming about, whatever you're believing for, know that God's dream for your life is far greater. He wants to supersize it. He's an overflow God. Ephesians says, "God can do exceedingly, abundantly above and beyond what we think." Why don't you take the limits off of God? You may not see a way, but God has a way. One touch of God's favor can take you further than you could go on your own in a lifetime. Be open to God's dream for your life and embrace the fullness of the blessing He has in store for you!

A Prayer for Today

Father, thank You for loving me and having such a wonderful plan for my life. Help me to see the great things You have for me. I declare You are doing exceeding, abundantly above and beyond all that I can imagine! You are supersizing my dreams! You are an overflow God! Show me Your way today as I keep my heart and mind focused on You in Jesus' Name. Amen.

Wake-Up Thought

This morning, if God were to show you where He's taking you—the favor, the promotion, the influence—it would boggle your mind. You may think you're not the most qualified. You don't have the personality or the talent. That's okay. You don't have to figure it out. If you will keep being your best right where you are, you will come into favor, promotion, and opportunity greater than you ever imagined. You won't have to go after it; it will come to you.

Don't Settle Where You Are

Today's Scripture

> "No eye has seen, no ear has heard, and no mind has imagined what God has prepared for those who love him."
>
> 1 CORINTHIANS 2:9 NLT

God did not create you to live a little life with little dreams, little goals, little passion, little influence, little house. God thinks big. He thinks abundance. He thinks expansive. He told the Israelites, "I am bringing you into a wide land, a spacious land flowing with milk and honey." God has something bigger, something better, something more rewarding in front of you. Don't get comfortable where you are. *It's easy to think, Well, God's blessed me. I'm happy. I'm healthy. I have no complaints.* That's good to always be grateful. You should learn to be happy where you are, but don't settle where you are.

God never performs His greatest victories in the past. They're always in the future.

Remember today, you haven't touched the surface of what God has in store for you. He's going to open doors you never dreamed would open. He's going to bring talent out of you that you didn't know you had! You're going to see explosive blessings that thrust you to a new level. Keep praying, keep hoping, keep believing, and don't settle where you are. Embrace the blessing God has in store for your future!

A Prayer for Today

*Father, I worship and praise You today.
Thank You for big dreams and visions
for my life. I am grateful for where You
have brought me, but I'm not going to get
comfortable where I am. I believe I haven't
touched the surface of what You have in
store for me. I trust that You are taking me
higher and leading me to increase, first in
You, and then in my influence in the world
around me. I declare that I will see explosive
blessing in Jesus' Name! Amen.*

Wake-Up Thought

*You can probably say that you've seen God
be good to you. God has blessed you with
health, a family, and a job. These are only
the beginning of God's provisions. You have
not made it into your promised land. God
will take you somewhere greater than you've
ever imagined. He has more joy, more peace,
more influence, more wisdom, more ideas,
more creativity, and
more good breaks.
Take the limits off
of God.*

Don't Just Pray to Become a Better Slave!

Today's Scripture

> "Therefore, say to the Israelites: 'I am the LORD, and I will bring you out from under the yoke of the Egyptians. I will free you from being slaves to them, and I will redeem you with an outstretched arm and with mighty acts of judgment.'"
>
> EXODUS 6:6 NIV

When the Israelites were in slavery, they were forced to make bricks all day long. They were given quotas that were almost impossible to meet. And at one point, Pharaoh got upset and had the supervisors take away all the straw they needed for bricks. They had the same quota, but they had to go find their own straw. No doubt they prayed, "God, please give us straw. God, You know these supervisors are going to get upset. We're not going to make our quotas." They had been pushed down for so long. They had such a limited vision when they were praying for more straw. In effect, they were praying to become a better slave. God said, "That's too small. I don't want to make you a better slave. I want to take you totally out of that bondage. I created you as the head and not the tail, the victor and not the victim."

Today, don't just pray for improvement in your difficult situation, pray for deliverance from it! See beyond your circumstances and let Him lead you out into the place of victory and abundance!

A Prayer for Today

Father, I praise and worship Your holy Name. Today I release a slave mentality. I pray and ask for Your complete deliverance from every form of bondage in my life. Help me to think the way You think and see the way You see. I declare that I am the head and not the tail, a victor and not a victim! Thank You for freedom all the days of my life in Jesus' Name. Amen.

Wake-Up Thought

Maybe you prayed, but you didn't get the promotion you wanted. You applied, but your loan application didn't go through. A relationship you'd enjoyed didn't work out. You may become discouraged and feel as though God has let you down, but don't settle and end up right back where you started, never making any progress. You're believing too small. The door closed because God has something better in store.

Enlarge Your Vision

Today's Scripture

*"Enlarge the place of your tent,
stretch your tent curtains wide,
do not hold back."*

ISAIAH 54:2 NIV

God has blessings untold prepared for your future! He has favor in your future like you've never imagined. He wants to take you places you've never even dreamed of. But in order for us to partake of all these blessings, we have to increase our capacity to receive.

Think about this: if you have a one-gallon bucket, and someone has fifty gallons to give you, the problem is not with the supply. The problem is that you don't have the capacity to receive the fifty gallons. But if you get rid of that small container and get something larger, you will be able to receive more. It's the same way with God. If we think we've reached our limit, the problem isn't that God doesn't have the resources or the ability. The problem is that our container is too small. We have to enlarge our vision and make room for the new things God has for us. Our attitude should be, *Yes, the economy is down, but I know God is still on the throne. I know that wherever I go, His goodness and mercy follow me.* When you enlarge your vision, you are increasing your capacity to receive so that you can take hold of the blessings He has in store for you!

A Prayer for Today

Father, thank You for Your loving care for me. Today I choose to believe in You and increase my capacity to receive. I let go of limited thinking and old mindsets. I am enlarging my vision and making room for abundance and blessings. I set my focus on Your Word and open myself to everything You have in store for me in Jesus' Name. Amen.

Wake-Up Thought

God wants this to be the best time of your life. But if you are going to receive God's favor, you must enlarge your vision. You can't go around thinking negative, defeated, limiting thoughts. To experience God's immeasurable favor, you must start expecting His blessings. Start thinking bigger. Get rid of any old negative mindset. If you will make room for increase in your own thinking, God will bring those things to pass.

Wait on the Lord

Today's Scripture

> *But those who wait on the LORD shall renew their strength; they shall mount up with wings like eagles, they shall run and not be weary, they shall walk and not faint.*
>
> ISAIAH 40:31 NKJV

D o you need strength today? Sometimes it's easy to get discouraged when you're constantly looking at the circumstances of life. You may feel tired and weary from a long spiritual or emotional battle. But when you wait on the Lord, the Bible says your strength will be renewed.

Waiting on the Lord means you're putting your trust and hope in Him. You're living with an attitude of faith and expectancy. In the natural, if you are waiting for a special dinner guest, you probably aren't just sitting around the house wondering what will happen. No, you're probably preparing for that special person, straightening the house, and making sure everything is perfect for their arrival. Most likely, you started weeks in advance making the menu and deciding what to wear! In the same way, when you are waiting on the Lord, it doesn't mean you are just sitting around. It means you are preparing for Him.

Are you ready for God to move on your behalf? Are you waiting on Him? As you take a step of faith, He'll meet you there. He'll renew your strength and lead you into victory in every area of your life!

A Prayer for Today

Father, I praise You for Your peace that passes all understanding. Thank You for Your promise to renew my strength. I choose to wait on You. I choose to trust You with an attitude of faith and expectancy. I declare You are leading me into victory in every area of my life! I choose to prepare for You to move mightily in my life in Jesus' Name! Amen.

Wake-Up Thought

God knew there would be times when we would feel battle fatigue. That's why He said, "There is a way to get your second wind. There is a way to have your strength renewed. Wait on the Lord." If you want your strength renewed, the right way to wait is by praising God. When you give God praise, you talk about His greatness; you go through the day expecting Him to turn it around. God promises He will renew your strength.

Hope

Therefore, since
we have such a hope,
we are very bold.

2 CORINTHIANS 3:12 NIV

God's Idea of "Big"

Today's Scripture

> The LORD has done great things for us, and we are filled with joy.
>
> PSALM 126:3 NIV

God did not create us to reach one level and stop. When we think, *Oh God, thank You that I've accomplished my dreams,* God says, "I appreciate your thanks, but I'm not finished with you. It's too small a thing for you to stay there. I have something bigger." In our minds, it could be huge. *Just got the promotion. Just moved into the Compaq Center. Just met the person of my dreams. God did more than I could ask or think.* The whole time, God's in the heavens saying, "You haven't seen anything yet. I'm glad you're happy, but that's a small thing."

God's idea of big is much different than our idea of big. In Scripture, David not only ended up serving the king, he became the king. He thought, *God, wow, You've amazed me with Your goodness.* God said, "Still, it's too small a thing, David. I'm going to put one of your descendants on the throne for the next thousand generations."

Remember, as long as you have breath, God isn't finished with you yet. He has so much more in store for your future. Be open to His leading because God's idea of big is so much greater than anything you could imagine!

A Prayer for Today

Father, I praise You that You have done good things for me and filled me with joy. Thank You for every good and perfect gift that You have blessed me with. I open myself to all You have for my future. I am enlarging my vision because You have more in store for me. I declare I haven't seen anything yet because You promised to amaze me with Your goodness! I believe and receive every blessing You have prepared for me in Jesus' Name. Amen.

Wake-Up Thought

The Scripture says, "It is your Father's good pleasure to give you the kingdom." God wants to give you the desires of your heart, but you have to have the faith of a child and be willing to ask. Quit asking small. Quit acting as though you're bothering God. Quit praying weak, get-by prayers. Your Father owns it all. He created the universe. If you want to see the fullness of what He has in store, you should learn to ask big.

Water the Right Seeds

Today's Scripture

> *"Still other seed fell on good soil.*
> *It came up, grew and produced*
> *a crop, some multiplying thirty,*
> *some sixty, some a hundred times."*

MARK 4:8 NIV

There was a report about children who had been bullied in school. It talked about how years later, those negative words were still having an effect on many of them. They interviewed this one man who was in his forties. He looked to be a bright, intelligent man, but he had not been able to hold down a good job, struggled in his relationships, and couldn't seem to get on course. He said that as a child, he was overweight. He was chubby, and some of the other children made fun of him and called him names such as "loser" and "failure." He made the mistake of letting those words take root. Now they were keeping him in mediocrity.

When somebody calls you something, either good or bad, that seed is planted in your soil. Now you get to determine whether or not that seed takes root and grows. When you dwell on what was said, you are watering the seed. You're giving it a right to become a reality. That's why it's so important that we're disciplined in our thought life. It's great when people tell you, "You're blessed. You're talented. You're going to do great things." Meditate on those throughout the day. Water those seeds and watch His truth become your reality!

A Prayer for Today

Father, I thank You for another day to praise You. I know You have deposited seeds of greatness inside of me. I choose to uproot every negative word deposited in the soil of my heart. I know they are lies and I will not believe them any longer. I choose to speak Your words of life! I declare that I am blessed, talented, intelligent, and creative! I am going to do great things for You in Jesus' Name. Amen.

Wake-Up Thought

All through the Bible, we find the principle of sowing, watering, and reaping of our words and thoughts. Just as a farmer must plant and water right seeds if he hopes to reap a good harvest, we, too, must plant good seeds in our thought life through our words and water them by meditating on them. Make sure you're planting the right kind of seeds. You're going to reap fruit from the exact seeds that you've been sowing and watering.

Believe God over the "Experts"

Today's Scripture

> But God hath chosen the foolish things of the world to confound the wise; and God hath chosen the weak things of the world to confound the things which are mighty.

1 CORINTHIANS 1:27 KJV

Did you know that according to all the laws of aerodynamics, a bumblebee should not be able to fly? Its wingspan is too small for the size of its body. It can't get enough lift. But here's the key: nobody told the bumblebee. It didn't get the memo. No experts were able to talk it out of flying. The bumblebee felt its wings on its sides and something in its DNA said, "I'm supposed to fly. I'm not made to just crawl around on the ground." It didn't read the latest engineering report. It just did what was natural and started flapping its wings and took off into the air.

Have you ever had the experts tell you, "You'll never get well; you'll never get out of debt; you've gone as far as your education allows; this is as good as it gets"? With all due respect, the experts can be wrong. The experts told Dodie Osteen that she had a few weeks to live, but thirty-three years later, she is still alive and healthy because God did a miracle for her. The experts told us Lakewood would never make it without the founding father, but we're doing pretty good! Believe God over the experts and watch what He will do on your behalf!

A Prayer for Today

Father, I praise You for Your goodness and faithfulness in my life. I believe You over what the "experts" tell me. You choose the weak things to confound the mighty! You use me in spite of my weakness. I believe what You say about me in Your Word. Thank You for the power of the Holy Spirit at work inside of me. I believe that You are faithful, and I expect to see Your goodness all the days of my life in Jesus' Name. Amen.

Wake-Up Thought

There is a popular country song that says, "Let's give them something to talk about." When the "experts" give you all the details of why you won't get well or be debt free, God wants to give you something to talk about. He wants to overwhelm you in such a way that everywhere you go you can tell your friends, your neighbors, your children, and your grandchildren about the great things God has done for you.

Pull Up Your Stakes and Press On

Today's Scripture

> I press on toward the goal for the prize of the upward call of God in Christ Jesus.
>
> PHILIPPIANS 3:14 ESV

Are there some tent stakes in your life that you need to pull up so you can press forward? Maybe you've stopped in a temporary place, and it's time to keep going. Maybe you've gotten comfortable and decided that your dreams are never going to come to pass. Your health is never going to improve. I'm asking you to pack up your tent, gather up your belongings, and start moving forward. You may have taken a temporary delay, but that's okay. That didn't stop your destiny. Today can be your new beginning. God is breathing new life into your spirit. He has greater victories in front of you!

Remember, the first place we lose the battle is in our own thinking. If you don't think you can be successful, you never will be. If you don't think you can overcome the past, meet the right person, or accomplish your dreams, you'll get stuck right where you are. You have to change your thinking. God said no good thing would He withhold because you walk uprightly. Get rid of a negative, defeated mentality. Make room in your thinking for the new thing God wants to do, pull up your stakes, and let God lead you into your promised land!

A Prayer for Today

Father God, I love You and praise Your holy Name. Today is my new beginning. I am pulling up the stakes of negative, defeated mentality and moving forward. Thank You for empowering me to pick up from this temporary place and move toward the dreams and goals You have for me. I declare that greater victories are in front of me in Jesus' Name. Amen.

Wake-Up Thought

The Apostle Paul kept his goal in front of him at all times. We produce what we continually keep in front of us. If you focus on an image of success in your mind, you're going to move toward success, but if you see yourself as barely getting by, your marriage getting worse, your health going downhill, then most likely your life will gravitate toward those negative situations. Keep in front of you the goals you want to see come to pass. That image will set the limits for your life.

New Thinking, New Living

Today's Scripture

> *"And no one puts new wine into old wineskins; or else the new wine bursts the wineskins, the wine is spilled, and the wineskins are ruined. But new wine must be put into new wineskins."*
>
> MARK 2:22 NKJV

Are you ready for increase? Are you ready to go to the next level, spiritually, physically, and emotionally? Many times, people hear that God has more in store for them and something resonates on the inside. Their spirit comes into agreement with God, but oftentimes their natural mind will be bombarded with doubt.

Thoughts will come such as, *It's not going to happen for you. You're not going to have a great year. You know what the economy is like.* Or, *You're never going to get well. You saw what the medical report said.* Or, *You're never going to get married. You've been single so long.*

Those are old wineskins; the old way of thinking that you have to get rid of. This is a new season. What's happened in the past is over and done. You may have been through some disappointments; you may have tried and failed, or things didn't work out. That's okay. God is still on the throne. It's time to get a new vision for your life. It's time for new thinking. You can't move forward with old mindsets. Let go of the old and embrace the new so you can receive all of the blessings God has in store for you!

A Prayer for Today

Father in Heaven, I honor You and give You all the glory. Today I choose to release old thinking, old habits, and anything that would keep me from Your best. Strengthen me by Your Holy Spirit so that I can live in faith and embrace the new life You have in store for me. I declare the past is over and done with. I am entering a new season! I am letting go of the old and embracing the new in Jesus' Name. Amen.

Wake-Up Thought

When Jesus wanted to encourage His followers to enlarge their vision, He cautioned them to not put new wine into old wineskins. He was saying that you cannot have a larger life with restricted attitudes. The good news is, God wants to fill your life with "new wine," and He wants to give you new "wineskins," new concepts, in which to contain it. If you will make room for increase in your own thinking, God will bring those things to pass.

Choose Faith over Fear

Today's Scripture

> *"This is my command—be strong and courageous! Do not be afraid or discouraged. For the LORD your God is with you wherever you go."*
>
> JOSHUA 1:9 NLT

Did you know that fear works just like faith but in the opposite direction? Faith opens the door for God to work in our lives; fear opens the door for the enemy to work in our lives.

The Bible says that fear has torment. Fear has no mercy. If you act on fear instead of acting on faith, it will keep you depressed, miserable, and lonely. So many people today are missing out on God's joy, peace, and victory because they keep giving in to fear. They feed fear by what they watch on TV or at the movies. They worry and dwell on all the bad things. Don't let that be you! The book of Romans tells us that faith comes by hearing the Word of God. The more you fill your heart and mind with God's Word, the stronger you will be so you can stand against the powers of darkness.

Remember, the power that is in you is greater than the power of fear. When thoughts come that say, *You're not able,* choose faith by saying, "I can do all things through Christ!" Choose faith today so you can overcome fear and live in the freedom and victory God has in store for you!

A Prayer for Today

Father, I praise You for giving me Your wonderful peace. I receive Your Word today that is life, health, and strength to me. I choose to close the door on fear by guarding what I say, what I listen to, and what I dwell on. I declare that Your power in me is greater than the power of fear! Fill me with Your love and faith as I meditate on Your Word in Jesus' Name. Amen.

Wake-Up Thought

Many people spew a litany of fear-filled ideas into their daily conversations, saying, "It's too big. It's been this way too long. It's never going to change." That spewing only opens the door to fear, worry, and doubt, and you'll feel weak, discouraged, and intimidated. Get in the habit of meditating on God's Word and dwelling on thoughts of faith, victory, and hope. You could see your whole life turn around today if you'd simply start thinking the right thoughts.

Move Forward

Today's Scripture

> Who redeems your life from
> the pit and crowns you with
> love and compassion.
>
> PSALM 103:4 NIV

We know people who feel that they've wasted years of their lives because of poor choices. They spent years in a relationship that was toxic, years with an addiction, years at a job where they weren't fulfilled. But you have to realize, nothing you have been through is ever wasted. Your past experiences, good and bad, have deposited something on the inside of you. Those challenges have sharpened you to help make you who you are today. When the enemy brings hardship into your life, God has a way of taking that experience and turning it around for your advantage. You may think you've hit a dead end, but if you'll stay in faith, you will see God begin to open up a new route. He'll put the right people in your path, the right opportunities, the right circumstances to move you forward toward the blessing God has in store for you!

Today, don't focus on what's happened in your past; focus on what God will do in your future. He wants to restore your soul and revive your dreams. Keep believing, keep expecting, and keep hoping, because God has a new route for your future!

A Prayer for Today

Father, I love You and come humbly before You today. I give You my past, present, and future, knowing that You will redeem my life. I let go of my past mistakes and failures. I release those who have hurt me. I choose forgiveness so I can be free to move forward in the path You have for me. I declare that I am not stuck because You are turning things for my advantage! You are restoring my soul and reviving my dreams in Jesus' Name. Amen.

Wake-Up Thought

Don't go around dwelling on your past mistakes. Nothing in life has happened to you. It's happened for you. Every disappointment. Every wrong. Even every closed door has helped make you into who you are. You may have encountered some great obstacles, but only because God has a great future in front of you. If you will get over what you think is a disadvantage, God will take what looks like a liability and turn it into an asset.

Shift into High Gear

Today's Scripture

> *"For the revelation awaits an appointed time; it speaks of the end and will not prove false. Though it linger, wait for it; it will certainly come and will not delay."*
>
> HABAKKUK 2:3 NIV

We're living in a day when God is speeding things up. What should have taken you a lifetime to accomplish, God is going to do in a fraction of the time because you honor Him. God is going to give you breaks that you didn't deserve. He is going to bring the right people across your path. You're going to see opportunities like you've never seen before. You need to get ready; you've come into a shift!

Think of it like a car. When you shift from second gear to fourth gear, the engine is still running at the same speed. It's not working any harder, but you're going faster. You're covering more ground. The higher gears have greater capacity. They're designed to go faster. In the same way, because you've kept God in first place, He is shifting you to a higher gear. You're going to go further faster, not because you're working harder trying to make it all happen, but because it's your time for acceleration!

A Prayer for Today

Father, I praise You for directing my steps and watching over my life. Thank You for Your hand of blessing and favor. Help me honor You in everything I do. I trust that You are working behind the scenes. I declare that You are causing me to go further faster because this is my time for acceleration in Jesus' Name. Amen.

Wake-Up Thought

This morning, be a believer and not a doubter. You may not see a way to your promotion or healing, but God still has a way. Keep God first in everything you do. Keep believing. Keep hoping. Your attitude should be: God, I'm in agreement with You. I believe You have shifted things in my favor. You are taking me further faster. I will accomplish my dreams sooner than I think. I will overcome these problems quicker than I thought.

Hold Your Peace

Today's Scripture

> *The Lord will fight for you, and you shall hold your peace and remain at rest.*
>
> EXODUS 14:14 AMPC

One time in Scripture when the Israelites were facing an impossible situation, God told them, "Hold your peace. Remain at rest, and I will fight your battles." Notice there was a condition, something the Israelites had to do. They were told, "Hold your peace." It's the same for us today. A command such as that indicates that something is trying to take your peace away: thoughts of worry, fear, or anxiety. You might think, *What if it doesn't happen? What am I going to do?* If you will just stay in peace, the Creator of the universe, the Most High God, will go to work on your behalf.

Remember, nothing can stand against our God. He has all power. He stopped the sun for Joshua. He closed the mouths of hungry lions for Daniel. Whatever you face in life, God promises He will fight your battles. Trust Him, remain at rest, and hold your peace!

A Prayer for Today

Father, I praise You because You are the Almighty God. Today I put my trust and hope in You. I receive this word and I choose to remain at rest. I hold my peace, knowing that You will fight my battles for me. I declare there is no God like my God! Thank You for working all things out for my good in Jesus' Name. Amen.

Wake-Up Thought

If you will trust in God, He will continually fight for you. It doesn't matter what you're going through or how big your opponents are. Keep an attitude of faith. Stay calm. Stay at peace. Stay in a positive frame of mind. And don't try to do it your own way. Let God do it His way. If you will simply obey His commands, He will change things in your favor.

Ascend

Today's Scripture

> Who may ascend into the hill of the
> LORD? Or who may stand in His
> holy place? He who has clean hands
> and a pure heart, who has not lifted
> up his soul to an idol, nor sworn
> deceitfully. He shall receive blessing
> from the LORD, and righteousness
> from the God of his salvation.
>
> PSALM 24:3–5 NKJV

You were meant to rise high in heavenly places. You were meant to stand with God above the cares of this life. But notice that this verse tells us that in order to ascend, we have to make sure we have clean hands and a pure heart. How do we have clean hands and a pure heart? First of all, only Jesus can make us clean and new. Once we receive Him as our Lord and Savior, we have to choose every day to stand against the enemy and his attempts to bring us back down. It all happens in our thought life. We have to guard our thoughts by guarding what we allow to influence our thoughts. We can't just watch anything on TV. We can't listen to any conversation. We have to make sure that what we allow into our minds is pleasing to the Lord, because what we allow into our minds will eventually affect our hearts.

If we are going to ascend, we have to have higher thoughts; we have to have a higher way of living. Choose today to ascend in your thoughts so you can ascend in your life and receive the blessings the Lord has in store for you!

A Prayer for Today

Father in Heaven, thank You for Your continued faithfulness in my life. Today I choose Your higher thoughts that bring life and strength. I choose a higher way of living in obedience to You. I refuse to be weighed down by the cares of this life. I desire to have clean hands and a pure heart. Help me to guard my heart and mind so that I can live a life that is pleasing to You in Jesus' Name. Amen.

Wake-Up Thought

It is usually the little stuff that gets us in trouble. Maybe it started with something we saw on the Internet, or someone said something unkind to us and we responded with sarcasm. Instead of asking God to forgive us quickly or letting go of the hurts, we quietly bury them deep down inside our hearts and minds and hope they will go away. But they won't. Don't let your heart get polluted. Be quick to be cleansed from sin and to forgive others, and the Lord's blessings will overflow.

The Time of God's Favor Is Here

Today's Scripture

> *That day the LORD exalted Joshua in the sight of all Israel; and they stood in awe of him all the days of his life.*

JOSHUA 4:14 NIV

What an amazing promise God gave to Joshua. He said, "Joshua, today I will begin to make you great in the eyes of all the Israelites." He was saying, "Today, I'm going to start releasing more of My favor, My blessing, My increase." But notice, there was a specific time in his life that God began to release favor in a new way.

God wants to do the same thing for you. He wants to release His blessing and favor in such a way that it makes you great—a great parent, a great spouse, a great leader, a great employee, a great friend, a great business person. He is saying to us what He said to Joshua, "This day I'm going to begin to make your name great. This day I'm going to begin to release My favor in a new way. I'm going to open doors that no man can shut." It is a set time of God's favor. Get ready! Make room in your thinking. Stay open to Him and keep an attitude of faith and expectancy because the time of God's favor is here!

A Prayer for Today

Father, I praise and worship Your holy Name. Thank You for pouring out Your favor and blessing on me. I open my heart and mind to receive every good thing You have in store for me today. I declare that this is my set time and You are releasing Your favor in a new way! You are opening doors that no man can shut in Jesus' Name. Amen.

Wake-Up Thought

When God selected Joshua to take over as leader of His people, He said to Joshua, "Just as I have been with Moses, I will be with you." Notice He didn't say, "Joshua, be just like Moses, then you'll be great." No, God said to Joshua, "Be who I made you to be, and then I will make you great." And that's all He expects of you as well. If you will be the best you can be, God will pour out His favor in your life.

Love So Amazing

Today's Scripture

> *Nor height nor depth, nor anything else in all creation will be able to separate us from the love of God which is in Christ Jesus our Lord.*

ROMANS 8:39 AMPC

Nothing can ever separate you from the love of God! His love is truly amazing. It goes beyond any human love we could ever know. There's nothing we can do to make Him love us more and nothing we can do to make Him love us any less. His love is true and everlasting.

Oftentimes, when people make a mistake or feel that they have disappointed God, they think they have to stay away from Him until they "get their act together," so to speak. But nothing could be further from the truth! He's always there with open arms ready to receive you and make you new. Remember, God's not mad at you; He's madly in love with you! You are on His mind day and night.

Today, if there is anything in your life that is keeping you from receiving His amazing love, set those things aside. Let His love restore you and make you new. Come to Him with an open heart and receive His amazing love and enjoy the blessings He has in store for you!

A Prayer for Today

Father, praise You for Your amazing love today. I thank You that nothing can separate me from Your love. I refuse to let my past or weaknesses keep me from staying close to You. I pray that You will help me overcome anything that is keeping me in bondage. I receive Your love today and invite You to make me new. Transform me into the person You created me to be in Jesus' Name. Amen.

Wake-Up Thought

Imagine that I'm handing you a one-thousand-dollar bill that is so crumpled and soiled that it's barely recognizable. Would you want it? Certainly, because you know it's still worth a thousand dollars. That's the way God sees each of us. We may feel crumpled and soiled, but we will never, ever lose the value that has been placed in us by the Creator of the universe. He loves us, not based on our performance, but on our relationship as His children. Nothing can separate us from His love.

Nothing Will Be Impossible

Today's Scripture

> *...now nothing will be restrained from them, which they have imagined to do.*
>
> GENESIS 11:6 KJV

In the Old Testament, the people were trying to build a tower to the heavens. The Scripture says, "Nothing they imagined was impossible to them." Their imagination was so powerful that God had to send confusion to keep them from accomplishing something for the wrong purpose.

That same principle is true today. If we can get our imagination working for the right purpose, if we will let God paint a new picture on the canvas of our heart and see ourselves as He sees us—strong, healthy, victorious—then we can rise higher and accomplish everything He's put in our heart. It may look impossible, but if you can imagine it, if you can see it through your eyes of faith, God is saying, "Nothing will be impossible to you." That means you can overcome addictions by forming a new image on the inside. You can break generational curses by creating the right pictures in your imagination. You can go further than you ever thought possible if you'll keep the right vision in front of you!

A Prayer for Today

Father in Heaven, I praise You for Your mercy and grace. Thank You for giving me the ability to accomplish Your purpose. I set my face toward You; I set my thoughts toward You. Paint a new picture on the canvas of my heart. I choose to see myself as You see me—strong, healthy, and victorious! I set my focus on Your purpose, knowing that with You, nothing will be impossible in Jesus' Name! Amen!

Wake-Up Thought

Your imagination is like a canvas. You can paint on it any kind of picture you choose through your thoughts, attitudes, and what you decide to focus on. Don't let doubt or fear paint on your canvas. Don't let "impossible" or "can't be done" thoughts blur the colors. Instead, take out the paintbrush of faith, the paintbrush of hope, the paintbrush of expectancy and begin painting a bright future on the canvas of your heart.

The Good Land

Today's Scripture

> For the LORD your God is bringing you into a good land—a land with brooks, streams, and deep springs gushing out into the valleys and hills.
>
> DEUTERONOMY 8:7 NIV

Are you facing an area of lack in your life? Lack in your finances, lack in your relationships, lack in your physical health? The good news is, that's not the place God wants you to stay! He wants to bring you into a new land with no lack, no shortage, no defeat, and no mediocrity. He wants you to live in a place where you will have more than enough so you can be a blessing to others. He wants to lift you up and keep you up. He wants you to remain stable and strong in Him.

The key is, in order to get God's results, we have to do things God's way. His love is unconditional; His access is unlimited, but our obedience is what opens the door to His blessings. We have to do our part and humble ourselves before Him and keep pressing forward with an attitude of faith and expectancy.

Remember, promotion doesn't come from people, it comes from the Lord. When we follow Him, He leads us into the land of blessing, the land of more than enough, the land of opportunity. Today, put Him first, follow His commands, and let Him lead you into the good land!

A Prayer for Today

Father, I praise You for Your goodness and faithfulness in my life. Thank You for the good land that You have prepared for me. I humble myself before You and desire to be obedient in every area of my life. I want to follow You as You lead me into the land of more than enough. Today I recommit my life afresh and anew. Help me follow Your commands and leading in every area of my life in Jesus' Name! Amen.

Wake-Up Thought

The Bible says that if you are faithful in the little things, God will give you greater things. God rewards those who seek after Him. If you have been faithful in obscurity, faithful through the tough times, if you have given and served when no one was watching or caring, your payday is coming. God is about to release an abundance of favor that He already has in your future. When you remain faithful, God will promote you.

Keep the Right Things in Your Life

Today's Scripture

> *For as he thinks in his heart, so is he.*
>
> PROVERBS 23:7 NKJV

God created us as visual beings. It's so important that we create the right image in our minds, because the way we see ourselves is what we move toward. Visualization is simply seeing yourself the way you want to be. It's creating a picture in your mind of accomplishing your goals, overcoming your obstacles, and fulfilling your God-given destiny. Our imagination is extremely powerful. The way we see ourselves in these pictures that we create, over time, will not only drop down into our spirit, but if we continue to dwell on them, they get into our subconscious mind. Once something is in the subconscious, it's just like gravity; it pulls us toward it. All these internal forces are released, and more often than not, we become just like we've imagined.

If you'll create a picture in your imagination of something you want, a dream coming to pass, a business succeeding, a picture of yourself healthy and whole; if you'll keep that image in front of you, that's what you'll move toward. If you keep the Word of God in front of you, that's what will come forth out of you. Keep the right things in your mind and the right things in your life!

A Prayer for Today

*Father God, I love You and praise You today.
Thank You for creating me in Your image.
Thank You for my imagination and for
the ability to change my life by meditating
on Your Word. Help me to keep Your truth
before me always so I can walk and live in
the path You have for me. Help me to see
myself as You see me. I declare that I am
moving forward and You are bringing my
dreams to pass in Jesus' Name. Amen.*

Wake-Up Thought

*If we are going to become all God
wants us to be, we must win the
victory in our own minds. You can't
sit back passively and expect this
new person to suddenly appear. If
you don't think you can be successful
or restored, you won't be. But when
you align your thoughts with God's thoughts
and start to dwell on the promises of His Word,
when you constantly dwell on thoughts of His
victory and favor, you will be propelled toward
greatness, inevitably bound for increase,
promotion, and God's supernatural blessings.*

Walking Through the Storm

Today's Scripture

> *Even though I walk through the valley of the shadow of death, I will fear no evil, for you are with me; your rod and your staff, they comfort me.*
>
> PSALM 23:4 ESV

Everyone faces the storms of life. Sometimes we have the faith to be delivered from the storms instantly; sometimes we have the faith to walk through the storms. But no matter which route you take, you can be sure that God is right there with you. He will equip you and sustain you. He will give you the grace, the supernatural empowerment, to make it through.

Today, maybe you are facing a storm and can't quite see a way out. Maybe you're not sure what the answer is. All you have to do is take it one step at a time by saying, "God, I know

You have a good plan for my future." "God, I am doing better today than I was yesterday." "God, I know You are leading and guiding me." With every step you take, know that God is doing a work in your life. Know that He is with you, and He will comfort you. Keep moving forward. Keep taking those steps of faith and keep walking through the storm into the place of victory He has prepared for you!

A Prayer for Today

Heavenly Father, I praise and worship You today. Thank You for walking with me through every season of life. I thank You for being a shield of protection around me, for going before me and preparing the way. With every step, I know that You are doing a work in my life and working on my behalf. Keep me close to You and give me strength as I move forward into the victory You have for me in Jesus' Name. Amen.

Wake-Up Thought

Delivering faith is when God instantly turns your situation around. When that happens, it's great. But it takes a greater faith and a deeper walk with God to have sustaining faith. Sustaining faith is what gets you through those dark valleys and storms of the soul when you don't know where to go or what to do... but because of your faith in God, you do. Faith tells you the best is yet to come.

He Makes All Things New

Today's Scripture

> *And He Who is seated on the throne said, See! I make all things new.*

REVELATION 21:5 AMPC

When God puts a dream in your heart, when He puts a promise on the inside, He deposits within you everything you need to accomplish that dream. He wouldn't give you the desire to do something without giving you the ability to fulfill it. In fact, the Scripture tells us that God gives us the desires of our heart. In other words, He puts the desire inside of us and then works with us to bring it to pass.

Oftentimes people set out to accomplish their dreams, but they face a setback or disappointment, and then they feel as though their time has passed. But know today that no matter where you've come from, no matter what's happened in your past, God wants to make you new. He wants to give you a "do over," a fresh start.

If you feel as though you've missed opportunities in your life, if you feel as though your time has passed, remember that today is a new day. You are a new person, and God has new opportunities in store for you. If one dream has died, it's time to dream a new dream. He makes all things new in your life today!

A Prayer for Today

Father God, I praise You for Your loving-kindness in my life. Thank You for a fresh start today. I will not allow a setback or disappointment to keep me from moving forward. I know You are making all things new. I give You my past, present, and future and choose to follow the good plan You have for my life in Jesus' name! Amen!

Wake-Up Thought

When God gave you a fresh start in your life, when He breathed His life into you and made all things new, He did not do it so you could simply feel better for a few days. No, God is in the long-term new life business. But you can't move forward in your new life if you are stuck in the past. It's time to let go of past hurts, pains, or failures. Trust God to lead you straight through the barriers of your past and onto the pathway of new beginnings with Him!

You've Struggled Long Enough

Today's Scripture

> *"If a fellow Hebrew sells himself or herself to be your servant and serves you for six years, in the seventh year you must set that servant free."*
>
> DEUTERONOMY 15:12 NLT

All through life, the enemy tries to enslave us with a yoke of bondage—a yoke of depression, a yoke of low self-esteem, a yoke of compromise. He'll try to burden you down so that everything is a struggle. You may be working hard, but you can't get ahead because you have all these bondages controlling you.

Maybe you've been living with a yoke your whole life. It's been passed down to you. Maybe you don't realize it. You can't seem to get ahead. You're struggling in your marriage. Your children won't do what's right. Low self-esteem is all you've known. But God said to the Israelites, "I have seen the affliction of My people, and I am coming down to deliver them." God sees every yoke, every unfair situation, everything that you struggle with. He doesn't just sit back and say, "Well, too bad." No, He says, "I'm coming down to do something about it." You don't have to worry. The yoke destroyer is on the way.

God is saying, "I'm coming down to put an end to that struggle. I'm shifting things in your favor. I'm delivering you from addictions. I'm removing the bondage and setting you free to walk into the fullness of your destiny."

A Prayer for Today

Father in Heaven, I love You and worship You today. Thank You that the enemy has no power over my life. I am breaking off the yokes of bondage that have held me captive! I trust You are fighting my battles for me. Thank You for delivering me from all my enemies. I declare that I will stand and see Your goodness and freedom and victory in Jesus' Name. Amen.

Wake-Up Thought

In Deuteronomy 15, God gave the people of Israel a law that said every seventh year they had to release any Hebrew slaves. Every seventh year, if you were a part of God's chosen people, no matter how in debt you were, you were set free. All the pain, struggling, and suffering were gone in one day. God never intended His people to be held in bondage to anything. Get in agreement with God and affirm, "Yes, I'm coming into my seventh year. It is my time to break free."

His Call Remains

Today's Scripture

> *For God's gifts and his call can never be withdrawn.*
>
> ROMANS 11:29 NLT

When you think about your future, what do you see in your mind's eye? Maybe at one time you were excited about your life—you had big goals and big dreams, but you went through some disappointments or life didn't turn out the way you planned and now you've just settled where you are. Understand, God's plan for your life didn't go away just because you had some disappointments and setbacks or because somebody treated you unfairly. God didn't write you off just because you made some poor decisions. No, He knew every mistake you'd ever make; He knew every person who would wrong you, and He still called you. He still designed a perfect plan for your life.

No matter what's happened in your past, God's plan for your good remains. He still has a bright future in store for you. If you will get your hopes back and get your vision in line with God's Word, the rest of your life will be the best of your life! Keep standing, keep believing, and get a vision for your future because the Lord has amazing things in store for you!

A Prayer for Today

Father, I praise You for Your constant love in my life. Thank You for designing the perfect plan for my life. No matter what has happened to me, I know You are directing my steps and orchestrating every detail of my life. I choose to shake off the past! I choose to forgive those who have hurt me, and I choose to keep my eyes on You. Thank You for calling me and giving my life purpose in Jesus' Name. Amen.

Wake-Up Thought

The prophet Isaiah says, "No weapon formed against you will prosper." It doesn't say that we won't have difficulties or never have a problem. That's not reality. God said, "The problem may form, but you can stay in peace, knowing that it's not going to prosper against you." Because you're His child, because God has a hedge of protection, mercy, and favor around you that the enemy cannot cross, no person, no sickness, no trouble, no disability can stop God's plan for your life.

Hope

I pray that your hearts will be flooded with light so that you can understand the confident hope he has given to those he called— his holy people who are his rich and glorious inheritance.

EPHESIANS 1:18 NLT

Close the Door on Fear

Today's Scripture

> *And do not give the Devil an opportunity to work.*
>
> EPHESIANS 4:27 ISV

So many people today are living with less than God's best because they've allowed fear to creep in and take root in their lives. Fear is the greatest weapon the enemy uses to try to hold us back. Fear is not from God. Scripture tells us that fear brings torment. It's designed to paralyze us and keep us from God's blessings.

The good news is that God is greater than fear. His power in you is greater than any power that comes against you. But in order to walk in His power, you have to close the door on the enemy of fear. The enemy can't have access to your life unless you open a door and give him access. That's why we have to be careful about what we watch, what we listen to, what we read, and what we say. When we open ourselves to fear, we give the enemy opportunity.

If you've allowed fear to steal from you in any area of life, today you can be free—you can be finished with fear! It starts by receiving God's love and meditating on His promises. Meditate on His truth and speak His truth that sets you free! Surround yourself in God's love and let Him lead you into victory as you close the door on fear.

A Prayer for Today

Father in Heaven, I praise and worship Your holy Name. Today I come to You in faith declaring that I am finished with fear. Thank You for giving me a spirit of power, love, and a sound mind. I declare that Your truth has set me totally free! Fill me with Your peace and joy today as I worship You and move forward in victory in Jesus' Name. Amen.

Wake-Up Thought

Always remember: God honors faith; the enemy attacks with fear. Quit allowing any thoughts that create negative imaginations and fears to play destructive games within you. This is war! You must take those thoughts captive and then cast them out of your thinking patterns. Make a decision today that you will live in faith, not in fear, and that you will think on things that are pure and wholesome and of good report. If you will do your part, God will keep you in perfect peace.

He Has Another Seed for You

Today's Scripture

> *"For God has appointed another seed for me."*
>
> GENESIS 4:25 NKJV

In Genesis, Eve went through a great disappointment. Her son Cain killed her son Abel, which was the first murder in the Bible. I'm sure Eve, like any other mother, was devastated and heartbroken at the passing of her son. But we love what Eve said, "God has appointed another seed for me." In essence, she was saying, "I don't understand it. It doesn't make sense, but I trust God. This is not the end. He has appointed another seed."

When you go through things that you don't understand, it is not the end. Nothing is lost in the kingdom. God is going to appoint another seed, and that seed represents the future. It indicates what is coming. If you will let go of what didn't work out, let go of the hurts and pains, then for everything you've lost, God will appoint another seed. You'll give birth to more in the future than you've lost in the past. Keep praying, keep believing, keep hoping, because God is for you. Trust Him and embrace the good things He has in store for your future!

A Prayer for Today

Father, I praise You for Your mercy and grace. You are the giver of all life! You give life to my dreams, life to my relationships, and life to my mortal body. Today I choose to release the past and embrace the gift of life You have in store for my future. I declare that You have more for my future than I have lost in the past in Jesus' Name. Amen.

Wake-Up Thought

Every one of us has dreams and goals within our heart. There are promises we are standing on. Maybe you're believing to start a business or to be in ministry or for a relationship to be restored. Deep down you know God has spoken that to your spirit. He has birthed it on the inside, but you don't understand how He will bring it to pass. Remember that God is faithful. He has never once failed before, and the good news is He is not about to start now.

Reprogram Your Mind

Today's Scripture

> *Do not be conformed to this world (this age), [fashioned after and adapted to its external, superficial customs], but be transformed (changed) by the [entire] renewal of your mind [by its new ideals and its new attitude]…*
>
> ROMANS 12:2 AMPC

Many people today don't realize that the reason they're not happy, the reason they're not enjoying life is simply because they've trained their minds in the wrong direction. They've programmed their minds to worry. They've programmed their minds to complain. They've programmed their minds to see the negative. But just as we can train our minds to focus on the negative, we can also reprogram our minds to focus on the positive. It all depends on what we meditate on.

When we meditate on the Word of God, we reprogram our minds. When we meditate on God's goodness, we are developing a right mindset. When we choose to be grateful and focus on what's right rather than what's wrong, we are choosing a positive attitude. This doesn't happen automatically; you have to discipline yourself to focus on the right things. You have to make a conscious effort to spend time in the Word of God every single day until a habit is formed.

As you honor God with your time, He'll multiply it back to you. As you stay faithful and focused on Him, He will direct your steps and lead you to embrace the blessing and victory He has in store for you!

A Prayer for Today

Father God, I love You and praise You. Today I surrender my thoughts and mind to You. Help me retrain my thoughts so that they are in line with Your will for my life. I choose to have a positive attitude of faith and expectancy, and I thank You for empowering me to enjoy the good life You have for me in Jesus' Name. Amen.

Wake-Up Thought

This morning, set your mind in the right direction. Don't meditate on problems; meditate on the promises of God's Word. Victory starts in your thinking. If you will develop this habit of disciplining your mind to think the right thoughts and meditate on what God says, you will have more peace and more of God's favor and victory in every area of your life. You will overcome every obstacle and become everything God created you to be.

What's Chasing You?

Today's Scripture

> Surely goodness and mercy shall follow me all the days of my life; and I will dwell in the house of the LORD forever.
>
> PSALM 23:6 NKJV

In the Bible, David was known as a man after God's own heart. What kind of attitude did he have? Here in Psalm 23, he says, "Goodness and mercy are following me." David lived with an attitude of expectancy. One translation says, "God's kindness chases me everywhere that I go." David's attitude was that *something good is going to happen to me. Everywhere I go, I know God's blessings are chasing me. Favor is following me around.* No wonder he saw God's goodness! No wonder he overcame his obstacles and accomplished great dreams. He knew good things were chasing after him.

Do you know what's chasing you right now? Not debt. Not failure. Not mediocrity. Not defeat. Not lack. Not at all! You are a child of the Most High God. You have been crowned with favor. You have been redeemed from every curse. God has set you apart as His own special treasure. When you look back in your rearview mirror, you'd better get ready because you have a tailgater! There's something coming toward you at a high rate of speed. You know what it is? Blessings, favor, supernatural opportunities, restoration, divine connections—God's goodness and mercy following you all the days of your life!

A Prayer for Today

Father, thank You for Your abundant grace and mercy. Today I look for Your goodness. I look for Your favor and blessings. I set my focus on You and declare that good things are chasing after me—favor, supernatural opportunities, restoration, and divine connections! Goodness and mercy are following me all the days of my life in Jesus' Name. Amen.

Wake-Up Thought

When you walk in God's ways, just like a heat-seeking missile finding a target, God will send blessings that chase you down, favor that overtakes you. Out of nowhere, a good break comes, and it's not a lucky break. Unexpectedly, a dream comes to pass, and it's not a coincidence. Healing is chasing you. Victory is coming your way. Like a magnet, you'll draw it in.

Greater Than You Imagined

Today's Scripture

> *"What no eye has seen, what no ear has heard, and what no mind has conceived—the things God has prepared for those who love him."*
>
> 1 CORINTHIANS 2:9 NIV

Because God loves you, He has supernatural blessings in store for you: increase, favor, good breaks, and supernatural opportunities. His dream for your life is so much greater than you ever imagined. You haven't seen anything yet!

You may have a dream to get well again or to be able to walk without pain, but God's dream for you is not only that you will walk, but that you be able to run and play like you did when you were a child. Your dream may be to just keep your marriage together, but God's dream is that your marriage would be happier, healthier, and more fulfilling than

you ever thought possible! Your dream may
be to just pay your bills and make it through
each month, but God's dream is that you have
an abundance, that you be totally out of debt,
pay your house off, pay your credit cards off,
and have so much overflow that you can be
a blessing to everyone around you! Get ready
because God has greater blessings in store
for you than you ever imagined. Open your
heart today and keep an attitude of faith and
expectancy, and you will live the abundant life
the Lord has prepared for you!

A Prayer for Today

Father God, I praise You for Your continued love and faithfulness toward me. Thank You for Your hand of blessing on my life. I know You have supernatural blessings in store for me: increase, favor, good breaks, supernatural opportunities. I open my heart and receive by faith all You have for me. Fill me with Your peace and joy as I put my trust in You in Jesus' Name. Amen.

Wake-Up Thought

God is extremely interested in what you see through your "spiritual eyes." If you have a vision for victory in your life, you can rise to a new level. But as long as your gaze is on the ground instead of on your possibilities, you risk moving in the wrong direction and missing out on the great things God wants to do in and through you. Your life will follow your expectations. If you raise your level of expectancy, you will enlarge your vision. This could be the day you see your miracle.

Imitators of God

Today's Scripture

> *Therefore be imitators of God [copy Him and follow His example], as well-beloved children [imitate their father]. And walk in love, [esteeming and delighting in one another] as Christ loved us and gave Himself up for us, a slain offering and sacrifice to God [for you, so that it became] a sweet fragrance.*
>
> EPHESIANS 5:1–2 AMPC

When people look at you, do they see your family resemblance? Perhaps in the natural, you have characteristics of your father or mother; maybe you have their eyes, or mouth, or mannerisms. We should also have the characteristics of our Heavenly Father. We should display His likeness. We should have His eyes, His mouth, and His mannerisms, too. We should study Him and imitate Him with the same awe that little children do as they imitate their earthly fathers.

The Bible tells us that God is love. We are never more like God than when we are walking in love—when we are being patient and kind; when we are extending grace and mercy and forgiving others the way Christ has forgiven us. When you imitate God, when you do things His way, you get His results! And God's ways always lead to life, freedom, and blessing. The more you imitate your Heavenly Father by walking in love, the more you will see Him moving in your life. He'll open doors for you that no man can close, and you'll see His hand of blessing in every area of your life!

A Prayer for Today

Father in Heaven, thank You for another day to praise You and live for You. I invite Your love to flow through me today. My desire is to be an imitator of You in every area of my life. Show me how I can represent You through my attitude, speech, and actions. I want to be a blessing to others and follow Your ways. Let my life please You so that I can be an example of Your awesome character in Jesus' Name. Amen.

Wake-Up Thought

The Scripture says "we are God's workmanship," which implies that you are a "work in process." Throughout your life, God is continually shaping and molding you. The key to future success is to not be discouraged about your past or present while you are in the process of being "completed." You may think you have a long way to go, but you need to look back at how far you've already come and be encouraged. You may not be everything you want to be, but thank God that you're not what you used to be.

Hope

So prepare your minds for action and exercise self-control. Put all your hope in the gracious salvation that will come to you when Jesus Christ is revealed to the world.

1 PETER 1:13 NLT

STAY**CONNECTED,** BE**BLESSED.**

From thoughtful articles to powerful blogs, podcasts and more, JoelOsteen.com is full of inspirations that will give you encouragement and confidence in your daily life.

AVAILABLE ON JOELOSTEEN.COM

today's W RD

This daily devotional from Joel and Victoria will help you grow in your relationship with the Lord and equip you to be everything God intends you to be.

Joel Osteen
STREAMING

Miss a broadcast? Watch Joel Osteen on demand, and see Joel LIVE on Sundays.

Joel Osteen
PODCAST

The podcast is a great way to listen to Joel where you want, when you want.

CONNECT WITH US

Join our community of believers on your favorite social network.

PUT JOEL IN YOUR POCKET

Get the inspiration and encouragement of Joel Osteen on your iPhone, iPad or Android device! Our app puts Joel's messages, devotions and more at your fingertips.

Thanks for helping us make a difference in the lives of millions around the world.